Praise for *The Listening Leader*

*'If everything seems to be going too fast, if i........ ......, ...
grab this book, go off to a quiet corner, read some and you'll
feel calmer. It reconnects the decent ones among us to things
we always knew, but here is the hugely powerful evidence that
we've been right, and the clear ways we can do it even better.
Let's hope the bad guys don't get anywhere near a copy.'*

**Anne Scoular, faculty member,
former diplomat and international banker, psychologist
and writer, co-founder, Meyler Campbell**

*'It might be an inconvenient truth for some: successful leaders
have to be more than great managers. Communicative
leadership, as shown in this excellent book, leads you there.'*

**Joachim Faber, Chairman, Deutsche Börse AG
(German Stock Exchange)**

*'An excellent book offering a powerful and courageous new
leadership approach – highly recommend for any CEO who
wants to make a difference.'*

**Klaus Rosenfeld, Chief Executive Officer,
Schaeffler Group**

*'This book makes you never forget the most important learning
about long-term business success: trust building starts with
listening.'*

**Professor Dr.-Ing. Axel Stepken,
CEO and Chairman of the Board
of Management, TÜV SÜD AG**

*'The Listening Leader takes you on a journey into the future
world of communication in management. In a style that makes
for enjoyable reading, it provides an overview of the precondi-
tions for successful "communicative leadership": information,
communication, enabling, empowerment, action. Each aspect is
explored using real-life examples from the rich wealth of experience of a true professional in corporate communications.'*

**Mario Ghiai, spokesperson, corporate governance,
Allianz Deutschland AG**

'The book makes an interesting read for every communicator – but also for every leader. The most fascinating thing about it for me is that the great personality of Emilio Galli Zugaro as exemplary communicator transcends from life into print.'

Judith von Gordon, Head of Media and PR, Boehringer Ingelheim

'As Peter Drucker famously said: "Management is about doing things right - leadership is about doing the right things". Today leadership, more often than not, means rethinking the entire business model of one's company, requiring corporate executives to listen to all stakeholders in order to win a clear "license to operate" from society. This book is full of insights as to how leaders can get that right.'

Dr Paul Achleitner, Chairman, Deutsche Bank AG

'This book is fantastic: a must-read for corporate leaders seeking to navigate this new dichotomy where consumer confidence is low, but expectation for engagement is high.'

Edward Reilly, Global CEO, Strategic Communications, FTI Consulting Inc.

'How to be a successful leader in times of the social media empowerment of every individual is a tough call. This book gives guidance to young and old leaders, and the magic happens through an apparently simple trick: listen to your stakeholders to succeed.'

Maz Nadjm, founder, SoAmpli – an award-winning social selling platform; MIT Influencer, TedXster, and one of Forbes and *Sunday Times* Top 50 social media influencers.

'Emilio and Clementina Galli Zugaro provide simple rules and great stories to help leaders connect with stakeholders. To earn their support, you must start by listening. To understand how to listen – really listen – read this book.'

Roger Bolton, President, Arthur Page Society

'This truly generous book gives you a rare opportunity to learn from real cases of leadership successes and failures. Miss this chance at your own peril!

Rich experience, a lot of soul searching, and a true willingness to help managers do a better job on the part of a senior executive are powerfully balanced with the view of the aspiring leaders' generation. The book powerfully models the conversations that leaders of different generations should have together.

Warning and inspiring! After reading The Listening Leader *you won't have any excuse for not knowing what is expected of you in today's world. You will also know what you should work hard on!'*

Professor Konstantin Korotov, PhD, Associate Professor, Director of the Center for Leadership Development Research, ESMT European School of Management and Technology

'Understanding how to tackle the trust meltdown of recent years is the key challenge of current leadership. This book, that I have been looking forward to . . . argues that communicative leadership is one of the most promising ways to regain and maintain trust – by engaging stakeholders and empowering people. It is a must-read for senior management that will finally understand the true power of communication.'

Professor Lars Rademacher, PhD, Professor of Public Relations, Darmstadt University of Applied Sciences (Germany)

'As one of the great communications professionals in the industry, Emilio Galli Zugaro brings unique insights, emotional intelligence and personality to his work. At a time when there seem to be fewer examples of leadership to emulate, Emilio comes at the topic with exactly the right perspective. Pay attention to his thoughts . . . there is much to learn here.'

Dan Tarman, Chief Communications Officer , eBay

'An inspirational work. The Listening Leader *bristles with isight, common sense and practical tools for everyday use.'*

Paul Ramshaw, co-founder and CEO, sensation.io

The Listening Leader

Pearson

At Pearson, we have a simple mission: to help people make more of their lives through learning.

We combine innovative learning technology with trusted content and educational expertise to provide engaging and effective learning experiences that serve people wherever and whenever they are learning.

From classroom to boardroom, our curriculum materials, digital learning tools and testing programmes help to educate millions of people worldwide – more than any other private enterprise.

Every day our work helps learning flourish, and wherever learning flourishes, so do people.

To learn more, please visit us at **www.pearson.com/uk**

The Listening Leader

How to drive performance by using communicative leadership

Emilio Galli Zugaro
with Clementina Galli Zugaro

P Pearson

Harlow, England • London • New York • Boston • San Francisco • Toronto • Sydney
Auckland • Singapore • Hong Kong • Tokyo • Seoul • Taipei • New Delhi
Cape Town • São Paulo • Mexico City • Madrid • Amsterdam • Munich • Paris • Milan

PEARSON EDUCATION LIMITED
Edinburgh Gate
Harlow CM20 2JE
United Kingdom
Tel: +44 (0)1279 623623
Web: www.pearson.com/uk

First published 2017 (print and electronic)

ISBN: 978-1-292-14216-6 (print)
        978-1-292-14217-3 (PDF)
        978-1-292-14218-0 (ePub)

British Library Cataloguing-in-Publication Data
A catalogue record for the print edition is available from the British Library

Library of Congress Cataloging-in-Publication Data
A catalog record for the print edition is available from the Library of Congress

10 9 8 7 6 5 4 3 2 1
21 20 19 18 17

Cover design: Two Associates
Cover image: Arthimedes/Shutterstock
Print edition typeset in 9.5/13 ITC Giovanni Std Book by iEnergizer Aptara®, Ltd
Printed by Ashford Colour Press Ltd, Gosport

NOTE THAT ANY PAGE CROSS REFERENCES REFER TO THE PRINT EDITION

Contents

To Heidi, Fiammetta and Fabio

About the authors

Emilio Galli Zugaro is Chairman of Methodos S.p.A. Milan. He teaches communications and crisis communication at the Ludwig-Maximilians-Universität in Munich as well as courses at the European School of Management and Technology in Berlin on communicative leadership. He works as executive coach for top managers and entrepreneurs and as a mentor at the Entrepreneurship Center, München. He is Senior Advisor of FTI Consulting, Frankfurt. He has worked in communications functions in public service in Rome, and as a journalist for *Fortune, Wirtschaftswoche, l'Indipendente, Italia Oggi, Il Giornale, Finanz und Wirtschaft, The European* and others. From 1992 to 2015 he was the Head of Group Communications of Allianz SE. He is a member of Arthur Page Society.

Galli Zugaro is passionate about developing leaders, particularly those who are technical experts but need support with the people side of their role. He is seen as a thought leader in the area of communicative leadership, which focuses on enabling and empowering leaders and employees. His coaching style has been described as results-focused and honest, with a strong focus on listening, an understanding of the complexities of international operations and, especially, diversity and culture-related differences. His experience of businesses in Italy, Germany and USA is recognised as an important anchor for allowing him to address multicultural issues. He is not afraid to speak the unspoken and has created significant impact for senior leaders. He coaches in English, German and Italian, the latter his native tongue. He is also fluent in French.

Clementina Galli Zugaro, Emilio's millennial daughter, has an educational background in psychology and organisational psychology, having always been curious about people. Her work experiences in behavioural finance, consulting and in training and workshop co-facilitation attest to her ambition to understand people's motivations, the drivers of their actions and the interaction dynamics among them in order to improve performance and outcomes for all stakeholders.

Contact the authors: http://www.galli-zugaro.com/

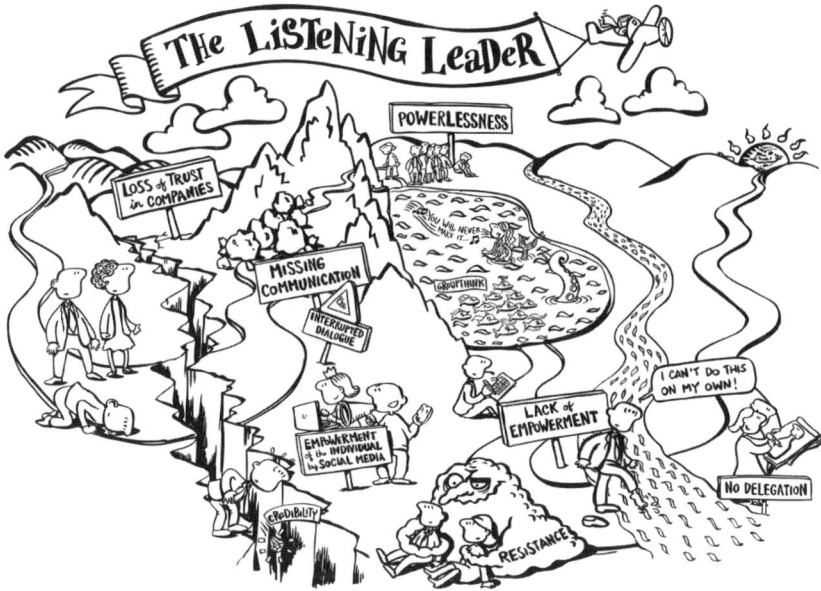

Introduction

Communicative leadership to succeed and the Listening Leader to enact and shape

- Corporations have lost the confidence of their stakeholders, who no longer trust them.
- Those stakeholders can withhold the license to operate that corporations need to do business.
- This has a negative impact on both their sales and their attractiveness as employers.
- Enabling you to succeed in the radically new social media environment through communicative leadership and becoming a Listening Leader.

This book is about tackling all the traditional tasks of a manager in a totally new environment, by using a different attitude in order to enthuse stakeholders in today's markets. It examines the philosophy of running companies nowadays, truly embracing stakeholders' expectations and finding a more efficient way of leading businesses to higher performance and sustainable and profitable growth.

I believe that we are in the middle of an erosive process for capitalism, which not enough players within the system have acknowledged, so far. I fear that companies are losing public acceptance at a speed they do not fully realise – yet. There have been two major developments that challenge the business world and therefore also its traditional leadership models: the loss of confidence in business organisations and the empowerment of citizens and consumers by social media.

But don't misunderstand me: this is not a book about how to manage. This small premise was prompted by my wife, who has also had management responsibilities. There are already plenty of good management books. All business schools teach best management practices; they are part of the curricula of business administration faculties around the globe and most large corporations offer very good management training in their corporate universities and training academies. That's why this book deliberately omits some of the basics, such as how to lead by objectives, how to manage a budget, how to run the daily business of a team in a corporation. You can find excellent literature and plenty of it on what traditional management involves, how to make tough calls on underperformance or how to climb the corporate ladder in a traditional corporation.

This book is addressed to all those who have an active interest in business at large and in leadership, specifically CEOs and other C-suite members (the chiefs in the top management, all starting with a 'chief': executive officer, financial officer, operations officer, technology officer, communication officer etc.), line and staff managers in large and small companies, HR and corporate communication practitioners, as well as those consultants and researchers who are interested in questions of leadership.

Readers will be offered a book written in plain language, filled with personal stories of leadership, failures and successes. It is not intended as an academic book, but it does take research into consideration. It should not bore you.

Who are we?

Emilio Galli Zugaro has been in charge of global communications at Allianz Group for 23 years, having previously served in politics and worked as an international reporter. Allianz, as shown by many indicators such as profitability and market cap, is the leading global insurance company with 140,000 employees working in more than 70 countries. It's one of the top five global asset management firms and is the largest institutional investor in Europe. Emilio now works as a business coach, mentor, author and consultant. He is Chairman of the change management company Methodos S.p.A. in Milan and Senior Adviser of FTI Consulting in Frankfurt.

Clementina, Emilio's eldest daughter, has a Bachelor of Science in Psychology from the University of Bath and a Master of Science in Work and Organisational Psychology from Maastricht University. Born in 1992, she is a representative of the millennial generation and will provide this perspective in each chapter (marked with a clementine fruit to echo her name). To do so, she has communicated with her network of other millennials to gather a broader range of 'generation' voices to challenge leadership. She has gained professional experience working in the Centre for Behavioral Finance, the assessment and development company SHL and the social media consultancy SoMazi.

The loss of trust in companies

In the past three decades we have witnessed a tectonic shift in the value of one of the most important commodities on the planet: trust. Some call it 'the trust meltdown'.[1] It affected all institutions alike but it was most visible in the loss of trust of people in the corporate world.

Edelman, one of the leading global PR firms, began to collect data from all over the world at the beginning of the twenty-first century, interviewing opinion leaders and decision makers and bundling their insights into the yearly Edelman Trust Barometer, a tool I have learnt to appreciate in the last decade.[2]

At the beginning of this millennium the big institutions (companies, governments, media) and their leaders lost their credibility edge to 'the average person' and the employees of a company, as well as to technical and financial experts. The normal employee of a company is more credible than the CEO of that company. And if you look at corporate information sources, the least credibility goes to the company's website, almost as low as advertising or public relations. So far, no big surprises – at least, not for me. What is surprising, though, is that the credibility of the CEO is almost as low as that of his PR officer and, even more surprising, the highest credibility is held by the average employee of the company.

An old adage says that trust takes years to build and can be lost in seconds. This truism, translated into business language, means that it takes years and millions or billions of investment to achieve strong brand goodwill and in the nanosecond of the loss of trust by capital markets those billions can be washed away by a steep fall in company shares.

Research also tells us what happens if people don't trust a corporation. Well, 48 per cent of those who don't trust a company would immediately stop buying their products and services and would advise their friends to do the same (see Figure I.1).

Figure I.1 Trust matters: Percentage who engage in each behaviour based on trust

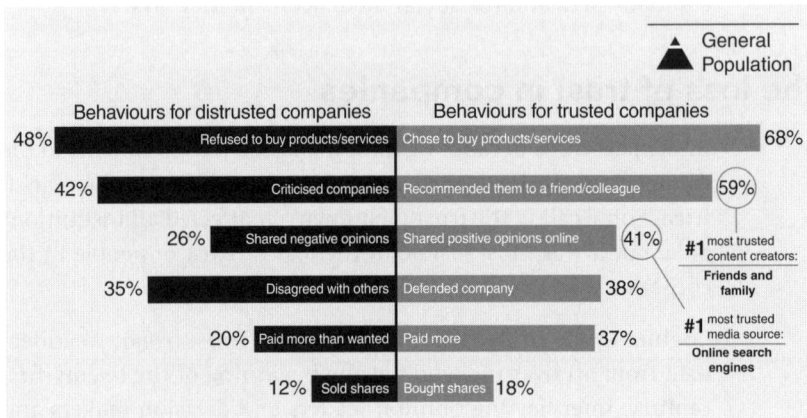

Source: courtesy of Edelman

The empowerment of the individual by social media

Imagine an airline passenger whose guitar has been broken by the airport baggage handlers. Picture him trying to get a reporter from a national newspaper on the phone to voice his anger. And then imagine this reporter writing a big front-page story reaching out to, say, 200,000 readers. Believe me, it's pure fiction.

What is *not* pure fiction is the story of David Carroll, a singer flying on a United Airlines flight, who saw his guitar being broken by the baggage handlers and who then produced and posted a witty video on YouTube. The clip featured his newly composed song 'United Breaks Guitars', telling the story of one year of fruitless efforts to get the $3,000 claim to be paid by United Airlines. So far, this video has been viewed more than 15 million times. This is without a journalist as a gatekeeper and with no chance for a United Airlines corporate communications officer to intervene and strike some smart deal with a reporter. David Carroll became the medium himself, without a TV station, a magazine or a newspaper.

TIME magazine started electing the 'Man of the Year' in 1927 and later it changed the name to the 'Person of the Year'. The Person of the Year in 2006 was 'You – Yes You – You control the Information Age'. *TIME* magazine acknowledged the emergence of the connected citizen who, simply armed with a computer, could embarrass politicians, corporations and governments.

Not only does it take just a second to destroy trust that has been built up over many years, it may also only take one person to trigger such an event. All that person needs is a smartphone or a computer.

If you take the two trends I just described, the conclusion is pretty straightforward. You have to connect to those who hold the power: the connected average citizens. The best channel through which to do so is not your CEO, your PR officer or journalists. You have to transform the only credible source of the company, its employees, into the most important source of the company. You need employees listening to stakeholders and driving their expectations into the company in order to change the company and create enthusiasm with all stakeholders. Only enthusiastic employees, customers, investors and public and private communities will recommend you as an employer, as a leader, as a product and service provider, as a stock to be bought, and as a credible corporate citizen.

This is what communicative leadership is about. Communicative leadership needs Listening Leaders to achieve the goal of enthusiastic stakeholders.

What does communicative leadership mean?

When I started to conceptualise what I've been doing for quite a few years, I came up with the term 'communicative leadership', to describe both a new way to interpret and enact corporate communications as well as a new leadership philosophy. We used the term, stretching it until the German sense of order overcame my department in Munich and I was asked to define communicative leadership, 'klar?' Defining things is a very German habit. Most meetings start by defining what exactly is meant by the content to be discussed in that meeting. I couldn't hide any longer so I came up with the following definition of communicative leadership:

Communicative leadership is the corporate translation of empathy and active listening. It describes the ability of a company to become a truly communicating organisation with an empathetic and outside-in culture which is able to listen to all internal and external stakeholders in order to drive decision-making processes and therefore ensure a constant transformation and adaption process.

Today I would add the following:

This transformation process improves the strategy of the company by involving stakeholders and securing their support. This support translates into the license to operate for the company. Communicative leadership is applied by the Listening Leader.

The Listening Leader

The Listening Leader is a courageous captain who guides the perfect journey to change and success. To do so she must master the five arts of (1) information, (2) communication, (3) enabling people, and (4) empowering people to (5) manage change. The result will be for her to be able to shape a truly empathetic business organisation, striving to grow by the enthusiasm of its stakeholders, who recommend the company for its products and services, as a sustainable investment, as an employer of choice and as a good corporate citizen.

The ten commandments of trust

You can only embark on the journey to communicative leadership if you as a leader and your company as a corporation gain or re-gain credibility and the trust of the stakeholders. Let's look at how to achieve this goal.

Andreas Bittl was the assistant of the Chair of the Business Administration faculty at which I teach in Munich's Ludwig-Maximilians University. Poor Andreas had decided to write his PhD thesis on trust. Only because his professor, the Chair for Risk Management and Insurance, liked (and owed) him a lot, did he allow him to choose such an apparently exotic, 'philosophical' issue for a business administration thesis. So, one day I asked him to translate his theoretical dissertation into civilised language. I added my little grain of salt and we boiled down 300 pages of academic phrasing into the ten commandments on how to re-establish trust. I take full responsibility for the reduction from Andreas' (now a successful manager) IQ to mine.

Here they are:

1. **Always set the example.** What would you think seeing your demure CEO after a town-hall meeting where he had sobbed, demanded blood, sweat and tears, and asked his employees to tighten their belts by two holes, reduce costs and yes, unfortunately also accept the lay-off of people, rushing off to the General Aviation Terminal, boarding the corporate jet,

snapping his fingers and asking the pilot to open a bottle of 1988 Krug Clos du Mesnil Blanc de Blancs and serving masses of Malossol caviar just flown in from Iran?

2. **Trust is based on a triangle made of competence, integrity and motivation.** Take away one of these elements and trust cannot be established. Or would you trust an insurance agent who acts with total integrity, is highly motivated to help you but unfortunately doesn't understand anything about insurance? Try to take out integrity or motivation and you'll see what I mean.

3. **EMMA.** An acronym created by the late Heinz Goldmann, a mythical figure in communication consulting. It stands for the four things you need to consider before entering any interaction with a stakeholder: an audience. E stands for empathy, the ability to step into somebody else's shoes. The first M stands for motivation. What is motivating? What drives your public? Do they want to learn, to make money, to build a network, to protect the environment? The second M stands for mentality. Who is your audience? Are they old, young, Germans, Aborigines, academically educated, healthy, disabled, male, female, Caucasian? A stands for analysis. Always analyse your audience. Find out as much as you can. If you can, ask directly and interact personally.

4. **Walk the talk.** Make your own position clear. Never lie. If you promise something, keep this promise. Don't commit to things you cannot fulfil. Remember that reliability is one of the main virtues of a leader and volatility may only be accepted for opera divas at a cocktail party not for leaders.

5. **Build and cultivate long-term relationships.** In many cultures family bonds, association with a tribe or a club allow us to establish trust quickly. In the business world interaction constantly occurs between people of totally different cultures. The only way for them to establish trust is to experience many fulfilled promises. Punctuality is one such test, a promise where respect can be immediately verified. It takes months and years to gain evidence of kept vows and commitments. More often, the more the proof of reliability has been given, the stronger credibility gets and trust can be established.

6. **Accept and admit mistakes.** The single most important thing parents can do to establish the self-confidence of their children and help them become strong adults is to be able to admit mistakes. Parents who pretend to be always right will never allow their child to grow confident. The same is true for politicians and business leaders who are unable to admit mistakes, understand and explain them and, if necessary, apologise. This is true strength.

7. **Have consideration and respect for partners, competitors and stakeholders.** When, in 2008 and later, US insurance giant AIG got into troubled waters, an American competitor bought advertising space to run a simple core message: 'Customers of AIG, come to us. AIG is in trouble, we are not, we're happy to welcome you as a client.' What a shabby thing to do, exploiting the stumbling of a competitor to humiliate them and gain business. Competition is absolutely necessary, but lack of style isn't. Not in order to gain trust.

8. **Accept regulation and feedback as necessary control mechanisms.** Who in a corporation longs for investigative journalists, internal auditors, visits by compliance officers, a spontaneous hello by regulators or, even better, a state attorney? Probably very few people. But would I ever propose eliminating one of these factors? Never! Because while I'm always looking at the glass half full, I am perfectly aware that there is an empty part in it, too. The evil of temptation that all people holding power have. The pressure of addictions that sometimes drives people into criminal acts. Or a simple joy of criminal energy, which also exists. To manage these very human shortcomings, we need control mechanisms and we also need real feedback on the important things we do.

9. **Say what you think and do what you say.** Don't try to manage different agendas, a public and a hidden one. Good managers are able to exercise their five senses to receive input *and* to focus on objectives. It is already challenging to consistently stick to an agenda. That's why it's better to simplify it as much as possible without losing the necessary depth. If you add an additional dimension, that is, a lie or a hidden agenda, you may confuse your priorities. And getting older it gets more

difficult to keep in mind different agendas. It's better to keep it simple and say what you think and do what you say.

10. **Treat others as you would like to be treated.** In corporate environments with very different cultural and religious sets of values it's almost impossible to agree on an extensive value set. I prefer to stick to the so-called 'Golden Rule'. The Fork Test story below may illustrate why.

These ten commandments to (re-)establish trust are the mantra of the Listening Leader, because the grease that oils the clock-work of good profits is *trust* – trust between stakeholders and the company, its managers and employees.

What would such behaviour look like in the real life of a young talent, a potential Listening Leader? Read this first story on the journey to becoming a Listening Leader.

The Fork Test

Years ago, Allianz used a bombproof system to select its highest C-suite potentials. Imagine in 1989 you were 29 years old, you graduated from an American Ivy League university, gained your PhD in Oxbridge, founded your first company which you sold with a large profit, you speak seven languages and you decided to join Allianz where you now manage a team of 130 people. Suddenly you receive a call from the PA of the Group CEO, somebody you've never met, who sits in the clouds of the Olymp, seven hierarchical layers above you. The PA invites you and your partner to a three-day stint in a farm owned by the company, somewhere in the beautiful Bavarian Alps. You are told nothing else, just the dates. Not why YOU have been invited and not your colleague next door. Not who is going to be there next to your partner, nor who the host is. Of course you imagine it's going to be the CEO, otherwise why would his PA be involved? You get nervous and you spend those three days in the beautiful countryside of Upper Bavaria, trekking, reading in the charming garden, being spoilt with excellent food from the regional cuisine. Then the final dinner comes and you find yourself with just nine other colleagues from all over the world with their partners.

Actually, who is the colleague and who is the partner? What you figure out is that there are also very senior managers next to the CEO and his wife. You get seated and the torture begins: you try to impress the C-suite member at your table. And now it dawns on you, why that smartass in your department hinted that you might have been invited to what insiders at Allianz called the 'Fork Test'. So you better behave well and show that you have manners and you thank your mum for having told you gazillions of times not to put the knife in your mouth. That dude from the audit department does it the whole time; you're sure he won't pass the Test. Then you're being sent to bed and the secret part of the Fork Test starts, one that we kept hidden from the candidates for decades. The best-kept secret at Allianz was that all the staff at the farm had a voice and a vote on the candidates at the debriefing session occurring after dinner: the gardener, the cleaning lady, the butler, the kitchen maid, the governor of the house. And if, in those three days as a guest, you had treated any of them in an arrogant way, you would have no chance of being promoted. And that bozo from the audit department who had been polite to all the house staff and treated everyone with respect would be a candidate for the C-suite, in spite of the fact that he put his knife in his mouth.

Because table manners can be taught, character can't.

The good candidate would convey her respect to every stakeholder, treat others as she would like to be treated, be empathetic and understand the motivation and mentality of the parties she interacts with.

Behaving accordingly to these three and the other commandments of trust in your everyday life as a professional will allow you to practise communicative leadership.

If communicative leadership is the art of perfect judo, leveraging the power of the stakeholders to succeed, the Listening Leader needs to train her body and mind with the ten commandments of trust and gain the skills that earn her the yellow belt of information, the orange belt of communication, the green belt of enabling, the brown belt of empowerment and finally, through her actions, the black belt of the Listening Leader.

Before we discuss what the role of the Listening Leader is in the greater scheme of communicative leadership, let me tell you my second story …

'Cancel all the contracts with our insurer!'

Sabia was standing at the departure gate in Düsseldorf, heading to Munich, when she suddenly overheard a man close to her shouting into his cell phone. That was unpleasant enough. But much more disturbing was what he was saying. He was profusely complaining about Allianz, the global insurance company Sabia was working for in Washington. This man was furious about her employer. He was asking to cancel all contracts with Allianz immediately and to make sure they never did business with Allianz again. Sabia was so embarrassed; she looked down at her clothes trying to figure out whether she was wearing her sports jacket with a rather visible Allianz logo. She felt personally insulted by the man's description of the service. She'd known her colleagues for 15 years now and she was saddened that this customer had had such a bad experience. Sabia was determined to set the record straight. When the plane was in the air she unbuckled, looked for the man and introduced herself: 'My name is Sabia Schwarzer. I work for Allianz in the United States and I couldn't help but overhear your conversation on the phone. Let me say that my colleagues in Germany would be very shocked if they had heard you – just as I was. The company you described is not the company I know. Can I have your business card and do something about your problem?' The gentleman, a CEO of a mid-sized company insured with Allianz, was baffled. It took Sabia three days to leverage her internal network until – with the support of very helpful colleagues – she managed to pinpoint the problem, indeed a screw-up by her employer, to have the issue fixed and the customer informed about a very fair solution to his problems. Her intervention won Allianz the business back. Sabia was working in communications in the United States; she was not a key account manager, she was not in sales, she didn't work in industrial underwriting, she didn't even work for the operative entity insuring the Düsseldorf businessman. She could have ignored the scene at the airport, shrugged her shoulders and said, 'Well, it's none of my business.' Instead, she took the initiative and gave her face to the anonymous corporation; she transformed herself into an ambassador for the company. That's how she got the business back: by listening; by communicating; by taking action; by taking up responsibility. An able communicator, empowered to represent the company. Years later Sabia Schwarzer was rewarded for her courage and her years of top performance by being appointed new head of global corporate communications at Allianz Group, leading a department she renamed CoRe, Communication and Responsibility. She is a Listening Leader practising communicative leadership. This book will enable you to become a Listening Leader too.

What seems to be just a singular behaviour can become a corporate attitude pervading the whole company. This can only happen if there is a clear strategy to enthuse customers and, especially, with a clear performance indicator that allows the management to drive virtuous behaviour that translates into the enthusiastic recommendation from one customer to a friend or family member, creating an avalanche of profitable growth.

Let's stop for a second on the concept of the recommendation of a company by enthusiastic stakeholders. There is a simple but very powerful idea behind this, an idea that helps us to tackle the challenge of the new world of lost trust and media-empowered citizens.

Recommendation by friends as the most acceptable growth path for business

One of the central issues being discussed around the world, from the Pope in his Encyclica 'Laudato Sí' through Ban Ki-moon and his UN Global Compact principles to Nobel Prize-winning economists and fertile think tanks on the planet is: Will economic growth continue? What environmental, social, political costs are we prepared to bear to sustain growth?

I don't have the answer to these questions but I believe in one thing: the only growth that will be accepted nowadays is the one that the trusted 'average person' will allow. It won't be the growth steered by central banks, governments, capital markets, corporations or trade unions. All of these institutions have suffered from loss of trust. People around the globe do not fully trust the establishment any longer, in spite of all the intelligent and responsible people employed by these very institutions.

Growth through word of mouth between people who know and trust each other will be the only accepted one. It is common-sensical, almost too easy to describe. And it's almost as easy to say as it is difficult to practise.

I have chosen to illustrate this point through the key performance indicator Net Promoter Score (NPS), measuring the willingness by customers to recommend your company to friends and family. It will be mentioned throughout the book and detailed further in Chapter 1 on Information and Chapter 7, 'Away with corporate communicators?'

Some smart people at Bain & Company, Boston, led by now Director-Emeritus Fred Reichheld, found out something apparently trivial at the beginning of the millennium: that the answer to one, very simple question, The Ultimate Question, would allow a company to predict its profitable growth through the willingness to recommend the products of a company, measured with an indicator called NPS.[3]

Is this a good reason for companies to divest from governmental relations, investor relations, fire the CEO, the whole communications department, the marketing and advertising people, salespeople and web designers?

Maybe. Find out more about the fate of these communications professionals in Chapter 7.

Has the certificate of death been filled in for governments, central banks, global finance and companies?

Of course not. These organisations are very powerful and they can determine the fate of corporations in spite of the fact that they have lost credibility. But because they lost credibility their fear of difficult decisions has grown and they increasingly chase consensus, and are starting to listen to the voice of the average citizen, the voter, the small investor, the consumer, the responsible and the environmentally conscious citizen.

It is all about regaining the trust of the average citizen and any way you turn it you need a trusted source to support your business. You need the support of your stakeholders to thrive as a company. But your weapons are getting rusty; the bullets of public relations fly only a couple of centimetres and no longer have any impact. The arrows of marketing and advertising are made of straw and wouldn't harm a soul. It's the word of your family member that matters, supported by independent and authoritative experts from academia and NGOs – the last remnants of the remaining credible institutions.

Personal, trusted recommendation is a growth factor that most would subscribe to.

This growth through recommendation generates *good profits*. A good profit is when the customer is happy to pay the price for the product. A bad profit is a profit extorted from the customer, albeit in a legal way. Take, for example, a telephone company where you have a one-year contract with a special discount for calls made out of your home town. Now your employer offers you a job in another town and you move. The first thing you do, after having put your books on the shelves in your new apartment, is to call your telephone company X and ask to switch the home-base from your old town to the new one. But they insist on the wording of the contract, stating that you had signed on for one year in your old town. You decide you hate them. You pay until the contract expires but there's another thing you do: speak about your experience with all your friends, 'real' and Facebook friends, too, swearing at the telephone company X. And there's one thing you never do again: business with that telephone company.

The money company X has made in the last month of your contract are bad profits.

Let's briefly recap: the companies as such (and also their CEOs) have lost the trust of their stakeholders. The most credible sources are average citizens and independent experts. Within a company the most trusted source is the average employee. The credible actions of the single employees translate into the company being recommended or not. The willingness of the customers to recommend the company can be measured. It is an indicator for good profits and therefore the future growth or lack thereof. Every employee is a credible spokesperson for the company and can drive or destroy growth with his or her behaviour.

If this is the case, and there's too much evidence for this to be ignored, the real question is: How then do you enthuse all the stakeholders, from your employees to your investors, the regulators, media, NGOs and the general public in this new world? And the answer is: through communicative leadership. By becoming a Listening Leader.

Don't be impatient – this is a journey. We learn through change and don't need to get lost. Every manager can become a Listening Leader. Every manager interested in having a career can draw the full benefits of this book, even more so if the company is in keeping with this philosophy and the more our reader is.

The purpose of this book is to help you succeed, to perform better and find a viable growth into a kind of leadership that is accepted by your immediate environment, including your private network. Growth of a business through the enthusiastic support of its stakeholders is a transparent game, challenged daily but resting on the pillars of trustworthy relationships with all those who have a say in the company's fate, insiders as well as outsiders.

Waiters in a steak-house?

We use the term *stakeholders* throughout this book. Who are they? For the sake of simplicity we cluster them into four groups: customers, employees, investors and society at large. We are fully aware that every company has dozens, even hundreds, of stakeholders. Agents, brokers, suppliers? They are both customers of the company as well as staffing the company's sales efforts. Neighbours? They are part of society as well as regulators, politicians, non-governmental organisations (NGOs), academia and all citizens interested for one reason or another in your company. We often find multiple stakeholders; I have been one myself for more than two decades: in my corporate experience I was an employee, a shareholder, I bought my company's products and pay taxes in the country where my former employer pays taxes.

The awareness of and the knowledge about our stakeholders, whatever we do in business, is highly relevant to achieving success.

Sometimes companies don't know their stakeholders. A cosmetic firm which carried out stakeholder analysis was surprised to find out that they were totally unaware of one of their top stakeholders: the community of hundreds of teenage make-up consultants running their own YouTube channel or blog, crucially important opinion leaders for the company's millions of young consumers.

Identifying and knowing your stakeholders is a key task for every leader. The map of stakeholders lies at the beginning of the journey to become a Listening Leader. You can identify them by asking yourself: who has an impact on my working life? It's your boss and your staff – that's clear. What if I don't have any direct contact with my company's customers because I work in accounting? Then my customers sit within the company: in all the departments my team interacts with. Find the time to map your stakeholders. The best sources are the stakeholders you already know. Ask them. If you have a corporate communications department, check in with them on this issue. There may be crises coming further down the road: you'll need to know who your stakeholders are. A new strategy could be developed for the company: your stakeholders should know about these developments. Your stakeholder map is like your Whatsapp group. It's your rolodex, your business version of your Facebook friends. Ideally you could press an icon on your smartphone and reach out to all of them. To do this, you have to find out who they are.

The ideal set-up of a company to fully benefit from communicative leadership

After establishing who your stakeholders are, next is to check whether you happen to work in the ideal company within which to rise to Listening Leadership or whether you have to change things from within, because your company isn't there yet.

Should you need to look for a company that has the right prerequisites for communicative leadership, here are some criteria:

- Does this company have a *clear vision, a strategy*? What makes it different to others? And, most important: Can people in the company relate their specific tasks to the strategy?
- Does this company have *leadership guidelines*, leadership values or – even better – a specific leadership vision?

- Does this company have one or, at most, two *KPIs for every stakeholder* and does it *link management compensation to all stakeholder needs*?
- Does this company *report* its achievements and failures in addressing not only its financial challenges but also its success or lack thereof as employer and in recruiting staff, in customer satisfaction or recommendation, and as a corporate citizen at large?

If the answers to these questions are all 'yes', this company is a likely candidate to adopt the concept of communicative leadership. In other words, if you want to succeed and choose to do so by becoming a Listening Leader, such a company is the ideal environment for you.

Why is a framework of this kind necessary to allow communicative leadership? This is because the true impact on profitable growth of a company is only possible where there is a minimum consensus on success of the company, being the fair distribution of enthusiasm between all the stakeholders and not just one or two.

The crises that threaten companies can be caused by any stakeholder: a boycott by customers can threaten a company's survival; a sale rally on your stock by investors can start the quick death of a corporation; regulators can revoke the company's license to operate; a walk-out of talents can kill the growth engine of a company. Threats can come from all directions and they are quick to cause perennial damage. But there are opportunities, too, potentially initiated by stakeholders. The company has to have a sensitivity, an awareness of the potential threats and opportunities coming from *all* stakeholders.

This is the necessary pre-condition to engage on the journey of communicative leadership. Only then can a leader tap the potential of her stakeholders to help drive the business.

The journey to become a Listening Leader entails four different achievements (Figure I.2), detailed in the following four chapters of the book:

> *The Listening Leader has to be credible* – this can be reached through first-class **information**.

> *The Listening Leader has to be able to constantly manage the dialogue with stakeholders* – top-notch **communication** will allow her to do so.

Figure I.2 The journey of communicative leadership

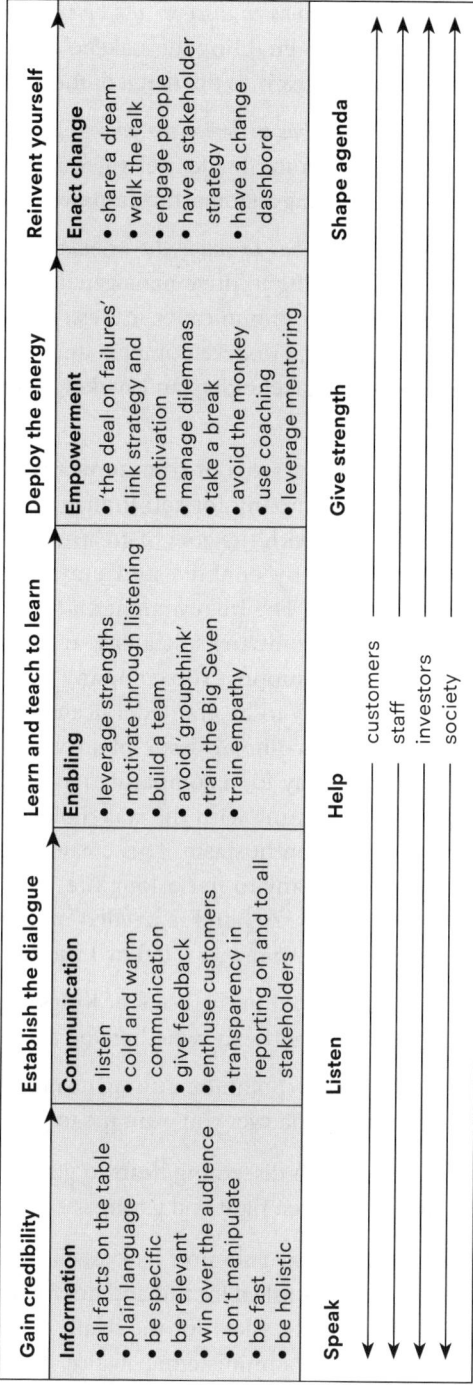

Gain credibility	Establish the dialogue	Learn and teach to learn	Deploy the energy	Reinvent yourself
Information	**Communication**	**Enabling**	**Empowerment**	**Enact change**
• all facts on the table • plain language • be specific • be relevant • win over the audience • don't manipulate • be fast • be holistic	• listen • cold and warm communication • give feedback • enthuse customers • transparency in reporting on and to all stakeholders	• leverage strengths • motivate through listening • build a team • avoid 'groupthink' • train the Big Seven • train empathy	• 'the deal on failures' • link strategy and motivation • manage dilemmas • take a break • avoid the monkey • use coaching • leverage mentoring	• share a dream • walk the talk • engage people • have a stakeholder strategy • have a change dashbord
Speak	**Listen**	**Help** customers staff investors society	**Give strength**	**Shape agenda**

19

The Listening Leader has to discover the energy of the stakeholders, groom it and grow it – **enabling** the stakeholders, foremost learning and teaching to learn, is the name of the game.

The Listening Leader has to deploy the power of the team and prepare for action – the Listening Leader delegates, hands over responsibilities, coaches driving an impactful **empowerment** of his people.

The Listening Leader has to shape the agenda and get ahead of developments – the ability to drive managerial **action** according to these principles of communicative leadership allows the Listening Leader to anticipate developments and shape the agenda, actively involving stakeholders and making them embrace and own the change.

The purpose of the five steps of communicative leadership is to prepare the whole company for self-managed action in a clear common framework, with the goal of creating profitable growth. Self-managed action by enabled and empowered employees multiplies the impact. The involvement and participation of all stakeholders in the company's strategy and actions creates a community that will support the company's public acceptance and allow the company to be granted a license to operate and to thrive. It may well become an issue of survival for every company. The only true way for a company to avoid life-threatening crises is for it to be in tune with the stakeholders and constantly work to deserve their enthusiasm. This creates the resilience that allows a trusted company to live a long life. And to achieve this very ambitious goal every hand is needed on deck: every single employee, every single manager – led by Listening Leaders.

There is a good story told in the Book of Kings (Chapter 3) and it seems to fit this book perfectly, whether you are religious or not:

The Lord appeared to Solomon during the night in a dream, and God said, 'Ask for whatever you want me to give you.'

Solomon asked for a discerning heart to govern the people and to distinguish between right and wrong.

God was pleased that Solomon had asked for this. So he told him, 'Since you have asked for this and not for long life or wealth for yourself, nor have asked for the death of your enemies but for discernment in administering justice, I will do what you have asked. I will give you a wise and discerning heart, so that there will never have been anyone like you, nor will there ever be. Moreover, I will give you what you have not asked for – both wealth and honour – so that in your lifetime you will have no equal among kings. And if you walk in obedience to me and keep my decrees and commands as David your father did, I will give you a long life.' So, Solomon got a discerning heart and the richnesses and long life.

(Book of Kings, Chapter 3)

So, Solomon got a discerning heart *and* the richnesses *and* long life. Think about it – it may be the right metaphor for the Listening Leader.

Introduction: a millennial's viewpoint

Business and leadership books are mostly written by white middle-aged men. And there's one good reason. Having dominated the upper echelons of business, academia and society at large, there are many of them with experience and knowledge to share. However, they are not the only ones. Thankfully, the world is changing and shifts are occurring regarding the diversity within companies and in other corners of society. It is immensely important to engage in conversations with each other in order to create richer knowledge together. It can add different perspectives and approaches to create a wealth of resources. One plus one equals three. I am here, a millennial woman, to wave the flag for my generation and the discipline of psychology within the context of corporate leadership.

What defines millennials?

Millennials already make up a big portion of the workforce today, and will grow exponentially within the next decade, permeating all levels and areas of business and society.[4] So, in order to understand the future of companies, we should look at what makes millennials different from previous generations.

Unlike previous generations, we don't have a unifying social revolution (such as the Vietnam war or the 1968 riots). Partly therefore, more than any previous generation, we are individualistic. Unlike previous generations, our communication and opinion sharing is online, global, instant. We know a little about a lot of things, often superficially.

Having grown up with societal circumstances shaped by the efforts of previous generations, we do not understand why certain things are still 'issues' (e.g. sexual orientation) and why other, infinitely more important things, are not taken seriously enough (e.g. the well-being of our planet).

Put your money where your mouth is: are companies and leaders really credible?

This is why, in our view, purpose must permeate every inch of the company. When we have the choice of working with like-minded people we should and we do. As the rise of start-ups attests, when this choice is not there, we create it. Of course there are limits to indulging these aspirations, yet there are also many unnecessary obstacles, which stem from previous conditions that no longer apply. Removing those barriers should be a no-brainer, yet often we as humans like to sit on what we know, defending it against all reason purely out of unfamiliarity with the new. But the new is not so new. There is simply a reorganisation of priorities and sensitivity for important issues, ranging from the responsibilities of businesses in the larger community, to the appreciation and nurturing of employees.

The challenger

My role here is to challenge assumptions and to provide complementary comments by reacting naturally to my father's ideas, as a female millennial labour market entrant with a psychological point of view. The same way it has, many times, occurred over a glass of wine or milk, depending on the period of time, over the past two decades.

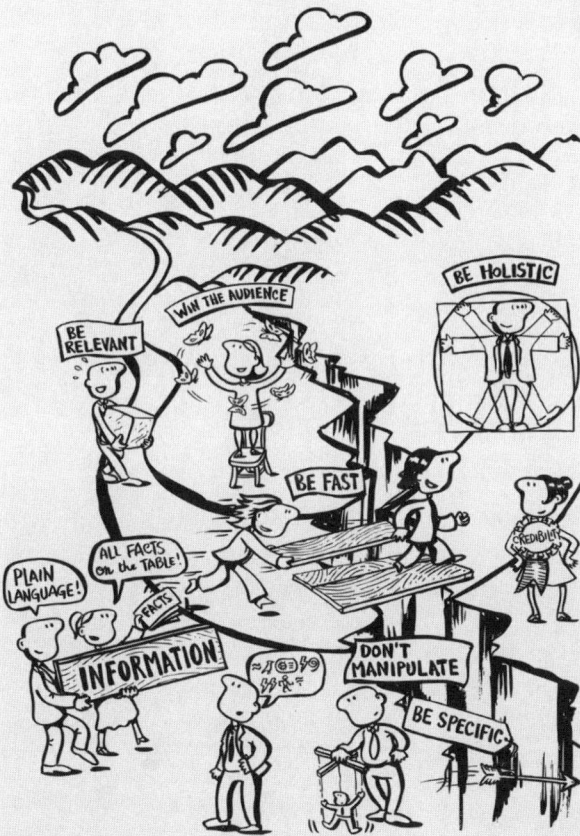

Information: How to get your message across and gain credibility

- What meaningful information means today and how to inform your public effectively
- The most dangerous mistakes and traps you are likely to encounter when providing information
- How information is gathered and shared
- What millennials perceive as best-practice information and how they gather it compared with generation X and baby boomers.

'I'm sorry, I don't know. I'm from another department.' Do you remember the movie *Around the World in 80 Days*? Phileas Fogg (David Niven) stands in his hot air balloon over a farmer's field and asks the Spanish peasant where they are. The farmer answers truthfully that the distinguished gentleman is in a hot air balloon over his field. This is a perfectly honest and true answer, and an absolutely useless one too.

Information has a function, a reason, a role. It has to fill the gap between ignorance and knowledge, between what I know and what I don't know. Information is normally conveyed through a message, through data, through facts. It seems to be an easy subject since we all instinctively know what information is, so no one really spends much time thinking about what damages or benefits bad or good information can result in.

But information isn't just generally important. It's the first of the five core disciplines a Listening Leader has to master. The Listening

Leader is excellent at informing, communicating, enabling, empowering and enacting change. The journey starts with meaningful information. Information lays the groundwork for establishing a trusting relationship with your stakeholders. Information has to be meaningful to justify the importance we give it. It allows us to gain the credibility necessary to become a Listening Leader.

Trust is a rare commodity. It's crucial to the functioning of our society. It is very difficult to achieve. You can't order it – neither in a shop nor online. You have to earn it. And meaningful information is the first step on this journey to trust.

To win the black belt of mastery in communicative leadership one has to honestly earn the yellow belt of information. It is not possible to bypass this step to become a Listening Leader, so better take the bull by the horns and learn, practise, excel in information and you will be able to reach the next milestone – good communication.

These five disciplines are not simply a technical purpose, they help paint the bigger picture. And that is about leadership. They are the disciplines that help you to create enthusiastic stakeholders, faithful, critical, involved and motivated stakeholders. This is a huge source of energy. It can help businesses to grow profitably over a long period, with an eye to the next generations – or what we would call sustainable business.

So, don't neglect an apparently easy discipline. It isn't as trivial as it may seem.

Having worked in an insurance company for more than two decades I came across a very frequent phenomenon in motor insurance. Whenever you have more than one witness account of a car accident it can be observed that for all the goodwill and trustworthiness of the persons, for every two witnesses you have three versions of the events describing the car accident. Was Driver A a blonde woman? Or was it a man with a ponytail? Every testimony could lead to a different assessment of the liability and has effects on amounts to be paid or not. That's why an insurer develops a sharp eye for precise information.

In daily corporate reality I have witnessed hundreds of misunderstandings based on inaccurate information. This is often the result of lack of training. The devil is in the detail.

Meaningful information can be learned, it can be practised and it can be improved. In this chapter you'll find some practical suggestions on how to turn bad information into good information. The red thread of the chapter is about reaching excellence in this discipline, everywhere you can. Every paragraph, every list, every example should help you to see where you can improve your information. It's about skills one can learn. And it's also about attitude and about values that you need. Because to practise communicative leadership you have to be able to rely on the trust of your stakeholders. And the first thing they have in their hands to measure your intentions and your quality as a leader is what you say and how you say it.

The CEO and information

'Why does a CEO need to be good at informing?' Because other-wise he may have to face early retirement. This book is not for CEOs (only) and not about CEOs (only). It is addressed to every person with an interest in leadership. But at least one paragraph here and there needs to be devoted to the top person managing a company. Whether in a governance system where CEOs are very strong (such as in America, France or Italy) or whether in a German corporation, where the law gives a management board the collective responsibility for running a company, the CEO matters. He or she is the figurehead, the good example stakeholders look up to. This person represents the whole company, personifies a brand. And therefore the chief executive officer has to be excellent in all the disciplines we discuss in this book (and in many more, of course).

A good CEO is a leader. A better CEO is a Listening Leader. And this means being a brilliant communicator. This peaks with his ability to listen – and you may want to read all about it in the next chapter. But it starts with the CEO's ability to master information. It's the famous 'tone from the top'. And you can't bypass it. This is where it all starts.

It's the CEO choosing how much information she is willing to share about the board decisions. Hers is the call on what to tell the stakeholders about the health of the company. It's the CEO who with the CFO determines when to warn the interest groups of an impending threat to the business. How the CEO informs impacts credibility of the brand of his company. It takes more than just occasional bad information to destroy a business. But it could take as little as one wrong sentence for you to lose your job.

This is what happened to a German CEO of a utility company. Rushing to go about urgent business in the restroom he was stopped by a cunning reporter who asked him whether his company was in negotiations with a certain competitor in another country. He truthfully said 'No'. The facts were that his company was indeed entering initial discussions with that company. But, according to German law in those days, 'discussions' and 'negotiations' were two distinct legal matters. And the company would have had to issue a public release on negotiations but not in the case of only vague discussions. Albeit pressured by his bladder, he said the right thing – according to German law. However, it was his bad luck that the holding company had just been listed on the New York Stock Exchange. And according to US law there is no distinction between 'discussions' and 'negotiations'. The SEC was immediately on the case of the poor CEO's holding company. They were fined US$500,000 and the unlucky gentleman had to resign. After he had had the liberating opportunity of going to the restroom. This is an example of where bad information resulted in a good man losing his job.

The role of information

Information has a *purpose*. Information is there to fill gaps, to share knowledge, to get the facts on the table. Not just facts but also feelings, figures, visions. All of it, basically, is 'data'. So, you can say, the purpose of information is to share data with others. The final goal is to establish a basis for a dialogue with the stakeholders, the audiences. And this dialogue should lead to trust. If you trust someone you will also be open to hearing difficult things and believing them or at least giving them face value. This all starts with fair, truthful, honest and authentic information, or what I call 'meaningful information'.

What is *meaningful information*, then? Let's learn from the professionals of information, the journalists. There are many good sources on what is best-in-class information. They sometimes don't seem to apply to the business world and can therefore become tedious for a business-interested reader. So, I make up my own priorities on what I think a Listening Leader should know about information. I'm sure there can be much more exhaustive lists.

I have four tips that I consider the minimum necessary to deliver relevant information:

1. Put all the facts on the table and repeat them.
1. Use a proper style and a plain language.
2. Be specific and relevant.
3. Win your audience's attention and tell a story.

1. Put all the facts on the table

The basic rule for writing a piece of news is to address the five 'Ws': who, where, when, what, why.

They help you cover the ground of your information. Tick those boxes to make sure you have all the basic facts together. To be good a piece of information has to be as complete as possible.

So make sure you get all the facts on the table.

This could look something like this: 'The change programme will start on 1 January (*when*) in all locations of our company, from the head office to all of our branch offices in the 23 countries we operate (*where*). Every single employee of our total workforce of 1,400 people (*who*) will be part of it. It will consist of the following four steps [...] (*what*) the goal being to grow our revenues by additional 10 per cent (*why*).'

The five 'Ws' are the basis of meaningful information, the skeleton.

Repetition pays off

People are distracted. They are distracted because information is everywhere and the selection of the relevant messages becomes increasingly difficult. So, even if a piece of information was successfully delivered doesn't mean it's been noticed, understood, internalised and pondered. It may just be forgotten or neglected. This is why Consul Marcus Tullius Cicero said 'Repetita iuvant' (repetitions help). And the purpose is clear: ensuring the reception of that message or piece of information. It's best to repeat messages in different channels, even if it seems a redundant exercise. But only multi-channel information can somehow guarantee that a piece of information really reaches the audience. So, do not hesitate to reiterate your content in emails, intranet, staff meetings and so on. At some point it will reach the minds of your people and stick in their memory.

2. Style – the how of information

How you shape content of the information will determine whether you're able to capture the attention of the audience and keep it. So, after having established the skeleton with the five 'Ws', put some flesh on the bones by looking at the style.

> The audit committee, consisting of five members of the top executive team, has examined all the relevant data concerning the gap analysis of the last two three-year plans and addressed all the implementation frameworks for the deployment of the internal and external synergy plans and will outline a proposal package for decision making to be submitted to the relevant governance bodies for a set of medium-term measures destined to impact the EBIDTA of our company by at least 5 per cent within the next planning period, to be added to the 3 per cent increase of EBIDTA already approved by our AGM in 2014. Consequences for the amount of full-time employees (FTE) cannot be ruled out at the present point and time.

When did you stop reading the previous quote? And if you were disciplined enough to read it and to try to make a sense of it, wouldn't you conclude that you may be fired short term?

We should be careful how we word our information. There is no 'one-size-fits-all' rule on style. And if we start discussing authenticity – which I consider rather important for being credible – we could spend long evenings debating different styles of conveying information. They are influenced by the provider of the information and his background, his age, his character, his education. Or our audience: whether we address a small community in a forlorn Scottish village or a global community of professionals scattered around 180 countries. And style is a question of taste, too.

On style we can learn from an authority who informs globally, at high-quality standards and has created a style of their own that also serves as a style guide for all of us who communicate globally, *The Economist*. So, use a proper style. *The Economist's*[1] style guide has seven rules to help us:

1. Do not be stuffy.

2. Use the language of everyday speech.

3. Do not be hectoring or arrogant.

4. Do not be too pleased with yourself.

5. Do not be too chatty.

6. Do not be too didactic.

7. Do your best to be lucid.

In other words: speak in the way you would speak to your teenage son. You respect him and take him seriously and you want to be treated with respect in return. You can't lie to him and you shouldn't. So, you say the truth in plain language. Don't use complicated language or bureaucratic jargon – he would look at you as if you were drunk.

English language

I'm not a native English speaker, but I love purity of language. I don't want to know how many wounds I have inflicted on the English language in my life and I apologise for every single one. A Nokia manager once opened a speech by saying: 'Ladies and gentlemen, tonight I'm going to address you in the world's most spoken language: broken English.' If you are an English native, please don't forget that the larger part of the world isn't and that everybody makes an effort to speak and write in today's most important language on earth, albeit creating linguistic monsters. And for those who aren't English natives and have to use this language, get some help to deliver the goods in a decent form. Both efforts won't be enough, though, because nobody can control whether non-natives even understand the correct use of the language.

I once sat on the Integration Committee that my company had formed. We were four managers representing the firm who bought the other and four representing the company being taken over. Everything had been smooth up to that point. My employer was the 'white knight' having saved this company from a hostile takeover by another competitor. We started to almost become personal friends after months of close cooperation during all the financial transactions leading to the takeover. Then the first day after the merger we had our first Integration Committee meeting and we started discussing matters of … integration. The acquired company needed to become part of a new, bigger entity and that was what we discussed. The first two hours were unusually diffi-cult; the atmosphere was tense. My CEO called a break and took me to one side. 'Something's wrong. Have you seen? It seems that suddenly the sunny sky of yesterday has turned into a hurri-cane.' I had become good friends with one of the four managers of the company we had bought, a Frenchman, like the other three. We spoke in French and when I called him to the side and asked him what was wrong, he said: 'Well, of course we are not amused. In the last months you guys all pretended to be our friends and now you speak of integration.' I must have looked pretty surprised. 'Integration,' he repeated, 'do you understand?' Then it suddenly dawned on me. The French word 'integration' has much more a flavour of 'conquest' than the more matter-of-fact meaning of the same word in English. Especially when it is used by Germans like those who were on 'my side' of the table. We were eight people, four French, three Germans and I, as an Italian. We all spoke in (more or less) English, none of us a native. We had at least three different perceptions of what that one important single word 'integration' – spelled the same in French, German and English – meant, namely slightly different things. There is no 'trick' to manage this difficulty. But we can be aware of the fact that there is not only 'pure English' on one side and 'broken English' on the other but also the misunderstanding of correct AND the misunderstanding of the incorrect English to make things more complicated. Is there a way out? Yes – ask or delegate. Ask locals in the different countries, native English speakers, the people in the communications department, in order to get a translation, be it 'linguistic' or 'cultural'.

3. Be specific and give evidence

Apparently there were times when a leader would say something and his audience would simply take it for granted. 'Big Joe said it, therefore it is true.' I'm 56, not old enough to have seen those times, if they ever existed. It is clear, however, that this no longer happens today. Today you can't be generic and be believed, not to speak of trusted. So, stating that 'our productivity is good' (or bad, that doesn't matter, here at least) is useless unless you are able to point at where exactly (in sales) it is particularly good and where (in IT) it isn't, what the general productivity is and compared to whom (competitors? all companies in all industries?) it is 'good' or 'bad'. So, use examples, such as sales and IT, in this case. If you state something, the likelihood of it being remembered and finally believed, depends on how specific you are. I learnt that adding crisp examples always helps the audience to understand a topic better.

'We truly believe in developing the talents of our people.' How many companies claim this? This piece of information will fade immediately, being so trivial and having been heard so many times. That person should have added: 'We hire only 5 per cent of our management from somewhere else; 95 per cent of our managers were normal staff members before we developed them into a managing position.' This sticks. And had she told me the story of Sally, the head of sales who had started as an intern in the marketing department seven years ago, who was then hired after her graduation and trained in sales, then sent to a branch office to sell her first products and then was made responsible for a large area, then felt she wasn't ready for management and had a setback, thought of dropping out, then asked to be sent to the corporate university to learn management practices, then was sponsored by the company in doing an MBA ... well, this would have stuck more. And had she called Sally on stage to tell her own story, in her own words, it would have been unerasable from my memory (see also the paragraph on 'warm communication' in the next chapter). Yes, because Sally is a very credible source of information when she speaks about her career. She is the best evidence to make the case that we truly develop our people in our organisation.

Be relevant

Think about whether information is necessary or not. You can fail in both extremes. In politics and journalism I knew what havoc sandbagging information could cause. That's an easy one. There can also be too much information, though. So don't overdo it. It is always helpful to cluster the information and make it as concise as possible, especially when it is not enormously relevant. Into a weekly email, call, conversation, town-hall meeting.

4. Win your audience's attention

When have you last seen an audience fully concentrating on a speaker, hanging on to her every word, no one looking at his or her mobile device, not a single spectator asleep or distracted? There is no longer such a thing as an audience where there isn't at least one person looking at his or her smartphone. Call it 'distracted listening', which is a first cousin of 'distracted reading', which is when you are reading on your PC screen and peeking at the LED-light of your android, while Bernstein is loudly competing with Abbado in the background and your three-year-old screams that he's built the most beautiful snowman EVER. You get what I mean.

And in order to 'break through' to your audience, you need to be interesting, easy to understand. To win the audience's attention there are also some technical points to consider.

One is the *source of the information*. If it is the boss providing the information, normally you get a good degree of attention – depending on how respected the boss is, of course. But her being the boss is enough of a reason to give the whole thing some air-time. Many more elements play a role, however, as we have seen. One of them is to always source your information, if you can. This will allow your audience to assess the credibility of that source, including your own if you are the source ('I believe we have to change how things are done in this department ...' will put the responsibility clearly into your turf). Basically, providing a source gives evidence to the examples, the statements, the facts and figures.

Another is the right choice of the tool. There are good practical reasons to send an email to let 400 people know something. You may save time compared to inviting them to a town-hall meeting, preparing a presentation, delivering it and sending everyone to work again. But the effects could be the opposite and might jeopardise the whole intention of the exercise of informing, if the given information is irrelevant. So, think about what medium you want to use for the information.

Tell a story

Tell a story if you want your messages to stick. So, what will actually stick? If you believe that what you said will be remembered literally, think of the witnesses of a car accident. There will be at least as many versions as there are people in the room. We know that people respond to the tone of the voice and the body language much more than to the content of what is being said. Whatever you choose to do, one thing is clear: it is easier to remember a story than sheer data. So, think of a good narrative, a good example, a proper story to make your message stick.

A story is able to speak to the gut, to convey emotions, to have a dramaturgy. It must surprise, shock, trigger reflection and thoughts. It may contradict prejudices, be funny, sad or simply memorable.

Every story has to have a plot with surprising turns, inspiring emotions; it has to have characters who are credible and authentic and it should have a meaning which can be moral or educational; or it can simply be funny or touch you.

See what The American Press Institute says about what a good (journalistic) story is:[2]

> Creating a good story means finding and verifying important or interesting information and then presenting it in a way that engages the audience. Good stories are part of what makes journalism different, and more valuable than other content in the media universe.
>
> Research proves two things about good stories:
>
> **Treatment trumps topic.** How a story is told is more important to the audience than its topic, what it is about. The best story is a well-told tale about something the reader feels is relevant or significant.
>
> **The best stories are more complete and more comprehensive.** They contain more verified information from more sources with more viewpoints and expertise. They exhibit more enterprise, more reportorial effort.

And what applies to storytelling in journalism is valid for all storytelling. Let's go back to Homer, the Bible or Shakespeare to learn about excellence in storytelling. The gist of it is: a good story moves you.

On *bad information*. To put the next points into one sentence: don't try to be too smart.

Here are the five biggest mistakes to avoid in informing.

1. **Don't be a spin-doctor.** Don't try to work around the truth. Very often I have seen managers taking decisions which they knew perfectly well would anger a stakeholder group. Then they helplessly or, often, rudely, turned to the poor PR person and asked her or him: 'Well, these are the crude facts. But, of course, you'll now turn it into a good positive story. The spin is what matters, isn't it?' No, the spin is not what really matters. What really matters are the true facts, the true feelings, the true figures. Admittedly, they have to be embedded into a story, into the larger narrative of the strategy of the organisation. But a story is not a spin, it's an expression. In business, a story should not be fiction. So, let's not mix up the two.

2. **Avoid jargon.** Information should not only be true but also credible (to be trusted). Credibility is not only assessed by the proven truth of the facts but also by language. So, don't invest too much time into wordsmithing, illusions, metaphors or diplomatic expressions or, worse, into business talk which is rightfully epitomised by the successful business game 'Bullshit Bingo'.[3] If you say – or write – the word 'synergies', everyone will understand 'cost cuts'. Well, if they are synonyms, you might say, you may as well use the term 'synergies' instead of 'cost cuts'. But not only would you not be sticking to the rule of expressing yourself in clear language, you would also lose credibility because it looks like you're hiding behind apparently meaningful words.

3. **Don't hide information.** Let's put fairness aside, for a moment. Or my call for honesty. Let's just look at the mere reality. In today's world, where even state secrets can be revealed easily through Wikileaks and similar platforms, there can no longer be any secrets. What was true in the past,

namely that secrets could only be kept if not told to anyone, is no longer true. One day neurology and technology will allow everybody's minds to be read and shared with the public. So, whether because of journalism or technology, because of Wikileaks or every single individual becoming a medium just by using a smartphone, the basic assumption every manager should make is: 'There are no secrets.' So, withholding information, 'because the times aren't ripe for this fact ...' just doesn't work. And the mere fact that you withheld known pieces of information at the point and time you informed will turn into the real crisis itself. So, get the information out, all of it. And quickly.

4. **Don't wait and see.** If you want to stay on top of the narrative and be credible, don't let others shape the information. Be the first to get the news out, if you own the information. If you are the first, people will recognise you for this. They will consider you the first and therefore most credible source of information. For the whole process of communicative leadership, but generally for all sustainable relationships, credibility is of the utmost importance. Without credibility there is no trust. And without trust you cannot motivate, move, drive, lead people and engage with stakeholders. So, make sure that you get the information out there as quickly as you can. Your information first reported by others is called rumour. Or gossip. Or speculation. So, if you want to avoid rumours, whispering at the coffee machines, people listening to the well-known bad-mouthers of the organisation, get the information out as soon as it is ready. Yes, I understand that reality may be different sometimes – approval rounds, double- and triple-checks often slow down the information process. But fight for speed, always.

Informing a second after the rumour is out is two seconds too late.

5. **Don't lie.** It is unbelievable what damage can be done with a lie. And don't think there's a distinction between small and big lies. Even a small lie can kill your career. My old boss Michael Diekmann, former CEO of Allianz, had a saying I've never forgotten: 'Small lies turn into big lies.'

One day such a little lie gave me a real headache. A newly appointed CEO of one of our subsidiaries had just written an email to a member of the local union who represents our employees in that country. Local employees had complained about a statement by that CEO quoted in a newspaper on the low productivity and lack of customer focus of our workforce. The paper quoted the CEO's statement made in an investor's meeting. And the employees thought this statement to be rather offensive. In an email to the works council representative the CEO wrote: 'And, by the way, the reporter who wrote this story lied, this quote is inaccurate, I've never said something like this.' Well, THAT was a lie. I knew that the quote was accurate, that there was a recording of that meeting and that an investor presentation contained a slide quoting the low productivity and the lack of customer focus of our staff in that country. Fortunately I was copied in that email and, even more fortunately, I had a very good working relationship with that labour representative. So I immediately called him to say that there had been a misunderstanding in the email that the local CEO would clarify in a personal meeting. He said: 'Your call was well timed. I was about to forward the CEO's email to the whole staff. I'll wait until I've talked to him.' Then I called the CEO and told him that it would have taken a nanosecond for this journalist to be called by one of our employees telling him the CEO had just called him a liar in an email. So, he would be wise to immediately call our union colleague, make an ample confession and fix this. Just imagine how long this CEO would have stayed in his job after wrongly accusing a journalist of misreporting . . . the reporter would have gotten a copy of that email in the turn of an hour by some disgruntled employee and he would have found an enemy for life. That CEO could easily have been ousted from his job just because of that stupid, unnecessary lie.

So, don't lie, don't beat around the bush and don't try to outsmart anyone. For most of the things you say, two mouse-clicks away, the truth can be found on the internet.

But why does information matter?

You may still ask yourselves, 'So what?' Is information really so important? This is something for HR or the internal communications staff in our PR department. I want to lead, inspire, motivate, envelop everyone with my charisma, when do we get to THAT? I, on the other hand, may feel some fatigue dealing with the issue of meaningful information because sometimes I was highly frustrated in my communication jobs to see how such basic things as an internal staff announcement would keep me busy fighting rumours, appeasing entire subsidiaries, adding another couple of hours to my already busy working day trying to mend some stupid mistake we incurred in internal communications. Meaningful information matters. It should be a requisite for every manager. It has to be for a Listening Leader. It is not to be delegated. Bad information may kill your career – or somebody else's.

The following situation occurred in a company where one of my family members worked.

The company wanted to go direct in their sales (it was a fast-moving consumer goods company) and hired a well-known expert in direct sales who had successfully managed the transition in another company. The staff announcement went something like this: 'As of 1 January, Lindsay McGregor will head the new Global Direct Sales Unit, directly reporting to the CEO, Susan Doodle. Let's welcome Lindsay who will be a great asset in helping us transform our company into a truly digital firm.' This company works in more than 20 countries and has very different sales channels, from small retail through affinity business (in this case veterinaries), department stores and, in some countries, through independent sales agents. Lindsay's task was to start an analysis on the countries that might benefit from an additional direct sales channel, since the company wanted to gradually adapt to the changing environment. But how the first message on his appointment was crafted was simply misleading for many, especially those who were particularly sensitive to the issue, such as the departments dealing with the agents or the retail partners. Would they be fired? Would their business partners in distribution be terminated in order to switch to direct sales? All hell broke loose in the organisation and poor Lindsay never recovered from where this careless announcement had left him from his very first day on the job. The whole organisation tried to make his life difficult and after two years he gave up and quit. And the company had a two-year setback that almost cost them survival. Also triggered by a bad piece of information. So, don't let fatigue catch you, a job may depend on it, maybe your own.

With this we have a good reason why meaningful information is important: because the bad use of information could cost you your job.

The Listening Leader has to master information

Why does meaningful information need to be an ingredient for the Listening Leader to keep her job? So far, it may seem like meaningful information is basically a tool to avoid disasters. And it is. Good information is the basis of risk prevention. This is because it helps in avoiding one of the most common reasons for crises: misunderstandings.

If you want to have a good laugh, look up an advertisement for Berlitz, a language school. It shows a young German trainee on his first duty in the radio station of the German coastguard. There comes an urgent call in English: 'Mayday! We are sinking! Mayday!' The young fellow, with a rather strong Teutonic accent, says: 'Here is ze Tcherman coastguard. Vott are you zinking about?'[4]

So, if I may come across somewhat defensive, there are good reasons for it. The first thing you learn in an insurance company is that risks can be very expensive and you learn to avoid them almost at any cost. And it helps. In business, in order to protect your customers and shareholders. And in communications, to avoid screw-ups demanding work-intensive clean-up. And as a Neapolitan I like avoiding sweat and hard work ...

But avoiding crises is not the only reason for providing quality information. Actually, relevant information is the prerequisite for you acting as a Listening Leader.

Meaningful information sets the tone of the conversation by providing fair, reliable, relevant and timely information. If you are fair you are more likely to be treated fairly in return. The communication with your audiences will become more matter-of-factly if you send all relevant information as a standard exercise, as comprehensive as possible and as curt as necessary. You will enjoy the reaction to your information if the audience has enjoyed what you sent them. And this is not about the positive content of the message, it's about the mutual respect that comes from an adult conversation.

Meaningful information is the basis for trust. Good information is about the truth: If what you said proved to be right and accurate, people will start giving you a chance as their leader.

Meaningful information is all about the timing. Providing the information when everybody had already heard a similar rumour at the coffee machine two weeks ago is poor. When what they hear is new they will listen.

And a Listening Leader has to be fair and respectful, reliable and on time. Meaningful information is the best basis for Listening Leadership.

The impact of meaningful information on business results

'Does good information have an impact on profits?' That's the kind of question one would assume the typical chief financial officer will ask. Actually, most of the CFOs I have known were pretty smooth communicators and dealt with information exactly the right way. And they wouldn't have asked this question. But, for the sake of argument, let's imagine a purely fictitious CFO who happens to be stubborn and powerful and who doesn't give a penny to your information philosophy, a CFO who adores crunching numbers and considers communicating leaders useless wimps. I know, it's difficult to imagine, isn't it? But this imaginary top-shot wants to know whether the share price will be moved by meaningful information or not. Well, if he knows his job he knows that *bad* information does indeed influence the share price. Actually, that's part of the basic knowledge set of a CFO. 'Misleading market information' can get you behind bars.

But what about the impact of meaningful information? I would be lying if I wrote that I have read the scientific evidence that there is a significant causality of good internal information on the share price. But I have some evidence that good employee engagement and profitability are correlated (read more in Chapter 7, 'Away with corporate communicators?'). And studies which show you how profitability drives the share price are in the gazillion.

Information is undoubtedly an element of business success. One of the gurus of profitable growth, Bain Emeritus Fred Reichheld, puts one of the key recipes to succeeding in customer enthusiasm in a rather assertive sentence: 'Even smaller companies must make a point of sending the right messages to managers and employees.'[5] As simple as that.

Meaningful information is the basis of good business.

How many times have you heard someone on the line in a call centre telling you 'I don't know'? Well, do you like doing business with such a company?

But constant meaningful information doesn't just provide growth, it also sustains the success over a longer period. In an interesting study on some very old and still very successful companies, the researcher Christian Stadler states that one of the key elements to allow these corporations to adapt to change is the ability to 'drive the organisation in one direction and speak with one voice. Mixed messages cause confusion.'[6]

The company's information

Excellent information is not a prerogative of individual leaders. Ideally it encompasses the whole company and allows for first-class information behaviour by this company's managers and leaders. Not only have the times gone when an employee would simply believe whatever his boss said. This is true for everyone, for every customer who doesn't trust the advertising, the website or the PR departments. The same goes for investors who want as complete a set of information as possible in order to evaluate the company. And the worst thing you can do is not to inform an investor properly. The laws that govern the financial information include jail sentences. And I've seen many shareholders' meetings where non-governmental organisations (NGOs), such as Greenpeace, Oxfam, Amnesty International and many others, engaged the management of a company for hours-long question times on what exactly the company did affecting the constituencies of these

NGOs. The demand for full transparency has increased enormously. More and more companies publish key figures relevant to all stakeholders.

What kind of information can this be?

I fly pretty often. What I'm interested in about the airline carrier I'm flying with is neither their return on equity nor their EBIDTA. I want to know whether this airline is safer than its competitors, what its track record in flying on time is compared to its peers and I'm interested in its service. I would love to read about this. But my daily newspaper only reports my favourite airline's profit and loss account. How boring (see 'Result for the customer' in Chapter 7).

Every company has four clusters of stakeholders: the employees, the customers, the owners and society at large. Within these four clusters you can place any specific stakeholder. Advice to all companies is: find out what your stakeholders want to know and give them this information. Meaningful information is provided in regular intervals; it is truthful, relevant and it enables the stakeholders to form an opinion on the company. The annual financial report should be complemented by a report on human resources, on the products and services as well as on the company's track record as a corporate citizen.

Just some examples for the four stakeholders of what may be interesting for them. Make sure this exercise is a good mix of facts, figures and good stories. But the facts have to be or become comparable with those of your competitors, as with financial data. This is why I won't expand the part on investors' information needs.

1. **The investors** need reliable, audited, financial figures as foreseen by the laws and beyond this, according to the regular exchange that analysts entertain with the company.

2. **Employees.** How many people work for this company? What has the turnover been in the reporting year? Split-ups by gender, age, nationalities. Data on recruitment, development and resignations. Results of the yearly employee engagement survey. And any other qualitative piece of information available that allows the strengths and weaknesses of this company's human resources to be assessed.

3. **Customers.** Any kind of key performance indicator related to the quality and the price of products and services. New products are interesting. Data on risks of the products, on speed of delivery, on product recalls.

4. **Society.** Just think of the audiences that make up this stakeholder: NGOs, governments, regulators, neighbours, the taxman ... Find out what matters to your public, deliver it and be the first to do so.

If you want a good example, go to the website of an online clothing outlet, Everlane (www.everlane.com). They have a policy of full transparency on the pricing of their products. You can find out where they manufacture each piece, how much they pay for the textile, for the tailoring, for the transport, the retail and what margin stays with the company. Amazing.

Don't forget two things you will read quite often in this book: let common sense guide you. And that one day all this information may be public anyway. No one has full control of even their own data anymore. So, you better check with your stakeholders what matters to them and deliver it, before someone else does.

If you think this is a cumbersome exercise, be aware that there are many companies that already publish an integrated report addressing all these items and many more. And in the global fight for trust those companies who inform their publics fairly, regularly and thoroughly are closer to victory. It would take a whole book to explain why and how companies have better odds of surviving and thriving if they excel at informing their publics. And fortunately this book has been written, by Bob Eccles and Mike Krusz of Harvard. It's called *One Report* and it's definitely worth reading.[7]

Meaningful information matters. It helps build trust with your stakeholders. It helps your voice get heard, because you say relevant things, because you use the right channels, because you don't lie. It's the first belt you will have earned to reach the next stage that leads to the next step, the orange belt, or improving your leadership and become a Listening Leader.

The next step is understanding your stakeholders. Taking them seriously. Listening to them. And doing something with what you hear. It's called communication and we'll look at it further in the next chapter.

The tools of meaningful information

1. **Face to face.** Personal meetings are the best way to provide information when the audience is small, the information relevant, if you seek interaction and if you want to appreciate and recognise your stakeholders and your team (and there are never enough opportunities to do this). A face-to-face meeting is personal and thereby shows recognition. It shows the relevance you attribute to personal information 'from the horse's mouth'. It allows for all dimensions of expression, body language, voice, eye-to-eye contact, all the gamut of expressions.

2. **Email.** Electronic mail is best when a larger group of people is defined (not generally all staff members of the company or all stakeholders), the information is somewhat relevant, has to be distributed quickly and when interaction doesn't come first.

   Ordinary information concerning a larger audience can be put in plain language and address the five 'Ws', reach the recipient in a second and create a level playing field of information for all those whom you want to inform. Have a clear and crisp subject heading. It should explain to the reader what the email is about at a glance.

3. **Newsletter.** Oh my God, another newsletter ... I'm not a fan of this tool, very honestly. Since most people have somehow grasped that 'communication is important' and most of them still think that sending messages to the world is communication, the use of newsletters in companies has increased. Every department, sub-department, project group and jogging society has a 'newsletter'. But we may need to swallow this pill. There are situations when a newsletter can be the best tool.

   Electronic newsletters add little value. It's better to build a page on the intranet and constantly offer pieces of information. You may find it more useful to use (push) email to create awareness and link to the intranet page.

   If you decide to publish a newsletter, make it a regular exercise.

▶

Make sure the newsletter is not just a sum of irrelevant pieces of news. Or, worse, 'the Boss's weekly sermon'.

4. **Employee magazine.** This is about storytelling. The employee magazine allows us to share information in a pleasant and illustrative layout, well-written, with in-depth explanations, using all journalistic formats.

   It doesn't really matter if it is printed or electronic, as long as you can reach out to all of your audience. If you have a team that doesn't work with smartphones or at desks (yes, conveyor belts still exist – though highly automated and run by fewer people than only a couple of decades ago) a printed staff magazine or paper is the better choice.

   As a journalistic product multiple formats are possible: the simple news piece, the news analysis, the report, the interview, the opinionated comment, portraits, regular columns, cartoons, significant pictures, explanatory graphs or charts and colours.

   The biggest benefit is that a magazine allows for best-in-class storytelling. The portrait of a successful staff member with an innate disability may motivate everyone to reflect on diversity, to discuss how everyone may tackle adversities, arouse more curiosity about a colleague, to have role models. The power of a good story is to move people. And emotions are a powerful result of meaningful information.

5. **The intranet.** A very common tool in many companies, the intranet allows for information to be provided to all the staff or to groups of people and departments earmarked on the intranet. But don't expect everyone to read it!

   Most larger companies have an intranet connecting (almost) every staff member. The better it is the more likely it is that the staff will read it. Making the intranet interesting is not much different from what it takes to make a staff magazine readable.

   The first screenshot of the intranet should always show the latest news at a glance. It has to be a relevant piece of information. And what is relevant is not just determined by the sender. You might think that what is being served in the corporate cafeteria as dish of the day is a trivial piece of information. Well, then keep your hands off any internal communication or management function in a large company. What the main dish of the day is really matters to most of that audience, believe me!

However, don't forget that the intranet is a 'pull' medium. You cannot be sure that everyone reads what you publish. This may be because they don't even regularly go onto the intranet.

Be aware: intranets are constantly changing. We see an increasing number of social workplaces evolving where staff members connect with each other, collaborate, share information and thoughts.

6. **Podcasts and webcasts.** Streaming is a sub-function of the intranet, but it's worth mentioning because it appeals directly and with impact to at least two senses, hearing and seeing. Moving images, music, voice and colours enhance the information and enrich it. Just ask young people how many of them follow tutorials on YouTube. Whether it's something trivial such as make-up lessons for teenagers or playing your favourite Eric Clapton song on guitar or even learning a language, one can find video tutorials on almost every topic. These tutorials convey information by adding the visual or sonoric dimension to a simple text. This stimulates more parts of your brain and is therefore more likely to be remembered.

And since you know how powerful common sense is, don't forget our five senses and their power to absorb information. Since you cannot use all of them (and I really don't know if I want computers or smartphones to convey olfactory information. Or would you really want to know how the horse's mouth smells?), make use of sound and image if it caters to the content of your information. Show the horse (and his mouth), so that everybody can say: 'I've seen and heard him really say that we all get a bonus!' And if the bonus doesn't come, well, pray God for a good explanation, like the aliens have kidnapped your CFO.

I cannot imagine an editor of a company publication not being interested in a good story, in relevant information. So, dare to ask for space in corporate publications. Because good corporate communicators know that their media become more relevant if they share the ownership with other colleagues, to the benefit of the audience.

Things to remember from Chapter 1, Introduction

Only a credible person can gain the trust of stakeholders. Meaningful information is the first step to establishing this credibility. To provide meaningful information you need to:

1. Put all the facts on the table.

2. Use plain language.

3. Be specific and provide evidence.

4. Be relevant and win your audience's attention by mastering storytelling.

5. Don't spin.

6. Be fast.

Meaningful information is rewarded by the company's stakeholders. The impact on the share price of good or bad information can be seen on a Bloomberg screen in a second. The same is true for the other stakeholders, potentially, only one click away from punishing or rewarding you for the quality of information you provide. Adapt the tools to your audience and don't expect the audience to adapt to the tools you use.

The CEO sets the tone from the top and has to excel in meaningful information, in crafting and presenting the narrative of the company.

A millennial's view on manipulation and freedom of choice: who are the deciders?

In their short centennial history corporate communications and marketing have produced powerful tales on the spinning and manipulating of information. From misleading ad campaigns to cherry-picked information fed to stakeholders, the industry is full of popular tricks ultimately employed in support of the company itself. It is therefore understandable that the general public demands transparency. And now, with increased information mobility, it is more possible to ask for it than ever. Yet how realistic is a Utopia, in which the stakeholder is fully and thoroughly informed of the ins and outs of the business workings, its finance, its products, its operations processes?

And with that I don't mean the overcomplicated legal statements, such as terms and conditions. You have an urgent need to book a flight and you have to tick the box to indicate that you agree with the terms and conditions. Now you have very little time and the conditions are 50 screen pages long I bet you don't read them. And even if you read them and there are consequences you might not like, between choosing the flight now that you need and not flying because one day you might be liable for something, you will probably decide to take the flight. Now the question is: Are we pretending to have an informed stakeholder? Or do we have an informed stakeholder? Or do we have a formally, legally informed customer who is not really enabled and empowered to be so?

A simple summary would be a wonderful and a true empathetic response to customers wanting to be enabled to make their decisions quickly and based on relevant information.

Despite growing pressure on companies to be transparent, many Fortune 500 companies still fail to provide stakeholders with complete financial statements.[8] Whistle-blowers and investigative journalism regularly expose companies who publicly say one thing and privately do another. The result is a disillusioned, sceptic Generation Y (and most certainly not just Y) with little trust. And, in the face of who calls us millennials apathetic and passive, I see non-budging attitudes and according actions. There is a general feeling that if you don't receive the information you care about from your business, you will find an alternative. And if there is no alternative, you will set it up yourself. After all, this is the era of the start-up and there have never been more new small businesses starting out than now.[9]

So, be honest, be transparent. What are the most important points I need to know? Then if one of these tickles my interest, you can lead me to where I can find more information. This goes for terms and conditions, but also product and process information, from the financial to the retail to the services industry. Not the vague buzzwords please. Real information.

Even with all information supplied, one might argue that inescapably customers and other stakeholders will be influenced by several factors in their decision making – marketing practices from product placement to adverts showing a desirable lifestyle next to a product aim to do just that. In his brilliant book *The Hidden Persuader*, Vance Packard illustrates the sobering reality of the use of psychology to manipulate people on a mass scale.[10]

Millennials are increasingly asking themselves: Have I had a say in this issue? Who has decreed that this product is what I need? Who has weighed the priorities within companies, but also as an economy? Who am I willing to entrust this decision making to, which then inevitably trickles down to me?

If we look at the Edelman Trust Barometer, the experts are scientists and researchers with a track record and a reputation with the present ruling class. If there is a peer group that punishes inaccuracy, fact- and number-fudgers, then it's the academics world, where universities and business schools aggressively compete for the best students, endowments and awards. While no academic finding can be blindly accepted as an alone-standing fact, the rigorous standards of science allow it to build upon itself creating a rich library of interlinked knowledge. Or do you think Nobel Prize winners are not credible?

Another characteristic that might grant you the label of expert is experience. By having lived through and dealt with the real issues you might argue that you are more entitled to credibility. Certainly this may be true in many instances. Nonetheless, experience is subjective and context dependent, so one single practitioner cannot speak for everyone.

The next category of people who might be rightfully entitled to decide for society are the citizens themselves. And in a way, that is what we do in a democracy. On certain issues that are deemed important enough, we all get a voice. However, for most decisions, our appointed politician of choice decides for us. Arguably, through the rise of social media, the average citizen has claimed back some control over the impact of his or her opinions. Millennials tend to trust the next person more than they trust experts.[11]

None of these and other categories alone can be thought of as the ultimate experts and the ultimate decision shapers. Each with their own mind-set and set of priorities and interests, they can only determine the best possible solution together through debate and exchange. Real communication.

This is something our generation hugely craves and thrives on.

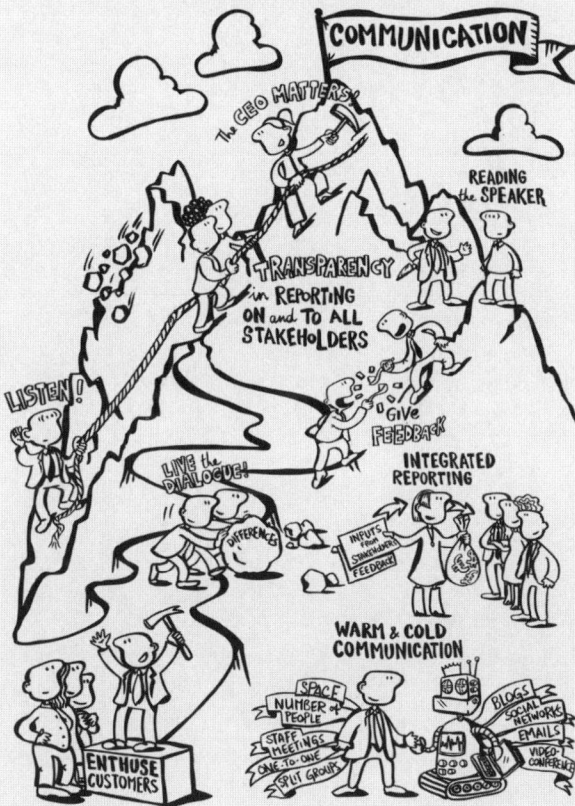

2

If I had kept my mouth shut, I wouldn't be here.

Sign under a mounted fish

Communication: Establish the dialogue

- The importance of listening in all its dimensions
- The power of feedback when it is properly conveyed
- How to deal with audiences of which we know little and how to establish dialogue even with large groups of people
- The key distinction between cold (technological) and warm (personal) communication
- Why communication with and among millennials is both so similar to and so different to communication within the older generation.

There are two big misunderstandings surrounding communication. The first involves the true meaning of communication. And the second is the total underestimation of the power of good listening.

What does communication actually mean? The biggest lie on earth, even before the careless words while one washes the dishes and says to his partner 'Of course, I love doing this, darling' is when a manager says: 'I communicate.' Normally by this he means 'I tell'. Whatever decision might be taken this manager would then say 'let's communicate', meaning that one would have to inform stakeholders about this decision. But this is not what communication is. Communication is a dialogue; information is a monologue. Communication is an *exchange* between people and organisations. It may lead to the adoption of the communicating partner's views (dialectic communication) or simply create awareness about two different standpoints after having listened to them and really understood, hopefully expanding the understanding (dialogic communication).[1] But it's an exchange where *both* parties listen and speak.

You don't communicate *to* somebody. Language is revealing. When I hear someone saying 'I communicate to ...' I know this person doesn't mean communication, but information. You communicate *with* somebody.

A new CEO learns to listen

Eva, a CEO I advised years ago, contacted me after her appointment. She sought advice for her communication strategy. She would start on 1 September of that year and the appointment was made public in June. So, she told me, she would run off her present job, hand over to her successor, take a summer break and start her new job. Her first question was about the '100 days of moratorium'. They are normally granted by the public to important people in business and politics before they go public with a statement on what they want to do – you may call it their strategy. Franklin Delano Roosevelt was the first to ask and get the 100 days. I told her that her staff, her investors and customers and even the regulator would be pretty upset if she only went to see them after three months. 'You're not Roosevelt and you have no New Deal to announce.'

'But what can I tell them?' she replied. 'I must get an idea of the issues on my desk, the challenges of the company. I have to get to know the most important managers, the board, before I can say something meaningful.' Of course she was right, and her remark showed me she took her job very seriously and didn't want to shoot from the hip. I remember that moment very well, because it was then that what I've always been preaching about communication gave me a simple answer to her rightful question. If it is true that communication is a two-way street starting with listening and only then followed by speaking, this would be the answer to her riddle. She would start by listening.

So we set up a programme that would allow her to engage with her stakeholders even before she started her new job. Not telling them anything but asking questions. What's wrong with our strategy? What's the first thing I should do? What's the most pressing short-term problem? Where should the company be in five or ten years? This would allow her to meet all the relevant people as soon as possible, showing them consideration and respect. And the most respectful thing we can do with our fellow human beings is to listen to them. Her first town-hall meeting was on her first day in the new job. And she introduced herself, said a couple of things about her persona and added: 'It's my first day on the job. Don't expect me to tell you what will change and what I'm up to, it's just too soon. Give me some time to address all important issues concerning the management of this company. First, I have to learn what our main stakeholders think about what should be done. And you, the employees of this company, are one of those decisive stakeholders. That's why I'm here today, my first day as CEO. So, let's use our time together, today. You know this company much better than I do. Now tell me: What's wrong with our strategy?' And for more than two hours she asked questions and got many answers. Some of them smart, all of them useful. She closed the town-hall meeting saying how much she appreciated the candour and that she would now continue her journey with the other stakeholders and by 1 December she would be able to answer questions. And she committed to holding a town-hall meeting on 1 December to share the strategy with the staff. In the meantime she would be happy to receive more input via email. And the story continues. But what matters at this point and time is to understand the power of real communication. This CEO became a very successful leader and now, retired, she is a mentor to many younger managers. Her success story was not caused by good communication, but it took off thanks to good communication.

I used this procedure many times afterwards. Some now call it 'Emilio's grid'. You can read more about it in Chapter 5, under 'The stakeholder grid'.

What really matters is that to become a Listening Leader you not only have to excel in information, the next belt you need to achieve is the orange belt – you need to master communication. No need to despair. It can be learned by everyone – introverts as well as extroverts. Or would someone doubt that introverts can be good listeners? Well, a good communicative leader is mostly a good listener. That's why I called him the Listening Leader.

Saying it with The Ramones: 'You gotta learn to listen, listen to learn.'

But when do we need to communicate?

The purpose of communication

Communication is one of the four important milestones that lead to effective action and change. If you want to change things you need to communicate. Communication helps you to understand your stakeholders. If you listen to them you will be able to constantly adapt your working efforts to the needs of the stakeholders you are serving. And you may bring these stakeholders along on your journey. Whether it's your boss, your internal customers in a company or the external consumer and client or a colleague. Communication allows us to both inform and to learn. And successful communication only occurs when both partners change after that process – either because they have learned something and can better understand the other person's viewpoint or because what you learned will make you change the things you do and how you do them. So, there has to be the will to change, the openness to accept and to listen.

The Listening Leader uses good communication to become a better leader, every day. Practising good communication means establishing a dialogue, creating the prerequisite for a structured listening process, followed by sharing this input and helping to modify the company's strategy accordingly. Only by knowing and understanding the needs of the stakeholders can the leader improve her own performance and that of her colleagues. She will understand where people need to be enabled to do a better job and decide to delegate and empower them in order to become agents of change. But you can only figure all of this out if you entertain a genuine communication, if you listen, and if you do something with it.

All relevant strategy experts, from Pericles to von Clausewitz and from von Moltke to Henry Mintzberg, note that strategy is a flexible thing, that you both need a vision of where you want to go and the adaptability to re-tune, fine tune, constantly challenge this strategy according to the context. And the 'context' is the stakeholders, normally summed up in 'the market', made up not only of the investors but of the peers, the customers, academia with its research, new talents on the job market or rules changed by regulators and legislators. The so-called perfect strategy followed through from A to Z as it was schemed and designed at the beginning, is normally simply the result of mystification in hindsight. The really perfect strategy is the one that leads to success. And this can only be obtained if you as a leader are open to accepting input for change. For this you need to master communication.

The purpose of good communication is to help you become a better leader and perform better, for yourself and for your employer. As you will have become stronger through the input of your stakeholders, your decisions will be more likely to be accepted by them, because they will recognise themselves and their own input in them. They will own your strategy as much as you do.

And for your stakeholders, being involved and co-owning a decision will make them more likely to grant you the license to operate, to grant you the legitimacy as a leader. If your stakeholders, your staff, your colleagues, your clients truly communicate with you they might be ready to accept you and accompany you along your journey, faithfully, critically and motivated.

And now, how to go about communicating? There are many different ways to entertain a dialogue so let's look at the most common ones in the business environment.

Why the CEO matters

The top manager heading the company is where all the interests converge or collide. The CEO is the last resort for the balance between the stakeholders' demands. She is the symbol of the appropriate balance between the stakeholders. She is responsible for exactly this equilibrium between the different interests. If she manages it to the satisfaction of both the stakeholders and the company she is successful and the company thrives. She has to be able to relate to all interest groups, to be empathetic with them. She is the Ombudsman of the stakeholders, the Court of Last Appeal. And she might lose her job if she loses their support.

It is therefore in the best interests of the CEO to lead the pack in terms of communication. Peter Záboji, a successful leader and

CEO and then teacher at the INSEAD business school briefly wrote: 'Modern leadership is mainly communication.'[2]

And a talent interested in a job should carry out a thorough check on whether the CEO is a Listening Leader. There are many ways to find this out. Look at the company's website and their annual report. How often is the customer mentioned? How many figures and how much information is provided on the performance of the company relative to customers? Is there any information on employee engagement?

Look for key performance indicators in the company's publications. I don't believe blindly in Robert Kaplan's 'You can only manage what you can measure', but most of those who are sceptical of what they – wrongly – deem 'soft-factors' do. And if you look at the shareholders' KPIs you'll find whole books on how to measure profitability. So, let's take them at their word: where in your publications do you address employees, customers and society, next to the investors?

Why is it so important to read about facts and figures on the communication between the company and its stakeholders? Because talk is cheap and verifiable facts are the best way to establish a basis of trust on the earnestness of the communication by the company. If this communication is earnest it will be based on true listening. The CEO has to prove that he's honest about listening and only reliable and verifiable data will show his or her commitment. Verifiable and verified, ideally by an independent auditor, like with the financial reporting.

'Warm' and 'cold' communication

I distinguish between warm and cold communication. Cold communication is technical, electronic or printed. It is an intermediated form of exchange, occurring through technical tools. The weekly conference call is cold communication. You can share information, you can ask and answer questions but you're not in a room with someone. One could say that normally cold communication stimulates only one sense, hearing or seeing, in our case listening to a person in a conference call or reading a text.

Warm communication is personal, physical. It appeals to two senses, sight *and* hearing. It allows for many more dimensions of communication that cannot be fully deployed in the cold communication: pauses, body language, tone of voice, volume of voice.

Both are potentially interactive and immediate (otherwise they wouldn't be called communication).

If one wants to qualify them I would say that warm communication is generally better than cold communication, because it can convey more emotions, it comprehends body language and is a holistic mutual listening experience. It is more personal. For large numbers, though, cold communication is generally the only fast way to go about having a dialogue.

Communication should not be a lonely event. It should become a habit, a constant exchange. The dialogue with stakeholders has a purpose as we have seen. So it's about a journey. And journeys allow for different means of transport: on foot, horseback, or by car, train, ship and airplane. A successful journey will integrate as many elements of warm communication as possible into a communication campaign. Even if cold communication might prevail, be as personal as possible. It may help to remember that a 'warm-hearted' person is more likely to be accepted than a 'cold-hearted' one.

Can you entertain a trusted dialogue with a large audience?

Personal communication has to occur in a place, in a physical location. So, the first limit is the space available. Even if you could use a stadium fitting 150,000 people you would have a limit to the people to communicate with. And, honestly, I can't imagine true communication in a large stadium. Consider that the largest of these buildings is the 1st of May Stadium in Pyongyang. You might agree with me that the North Korean propaganda wouldn't qualify as 'communication'.

Next to the space you also have the issue of the number of people you want to communicate with. I used to think that good communication was possible in town-hall meetings. I must say, experience has taught me this is not fully true. You can do it as an exercise of

▶

gathering opinions, as Eva did. You can entertain a rudimentary dialogue, you can exchange views, can ask and answer questions. You can make instant polls, let the audience co-decide on what you want to discuss, using votes by hand or tele-voting. Inserting elements of dialogue is always better than just informing.

What is possible with a larger crowd of people is to create a connection. Through appeals, rhetoric questions, closed questions (those whom you can only answer with 'yes' and 'no'), you can narrow the gap between you and the crowd getting simple answers through a vote, a clap of hands. But, honestly, how likely is it that you have to address 150,000 people and wish to engage them in dialogue? Well, should you be Kim Jong-un and rule North Korea, I apologise for not providing you with the answer. This book you're reading wasn't written for you, Mr Jong-un. The normal reader of these lines would rarely have the challenge of entertaining a dialogue with thousands of people on a hill or in a stadium.

The fact is, in larger groups you will not have a frank debate where everybody feels in a safe enough environment to air the full truth. It is difficult to make a statement that is not mainstream in front of hundreds of people. But it's this comment that would make the difference, just because it isn't mainstream. So, let's just accept that an honest and candid exchange is difficult and almost impossible in large groups.

An icon of listening, the author, coach and researcher Nancy Kline has said that, according to her vast experience, 12 people constitute the largest number for an honest exchange: 'Twelve is as big as you can make up a group and still expect it to be safe enough for people to say what they think. Organisations that gather 200 employees to announce policy changes and then open the floor to questions and comments from the audience are, in effect, not holding an open consultative forum at all. Most people will not stand up to speak in a group of colleagues that large.'[3]

It may not be a coincidence that at the Last Supper the party was made of 13, exactly one too many (Judas) for trustful communication ...

Once we have established that neither the stadium nor the town-hall meeting with 200 employees allow for good communication, there are still enough opportunities to engage in at least the effort to communicate warmly with your audience: staff meetings, one-on-ones, investors' roadshows, client meetings, open-door days.

And how do you reach out to more than 12 people if you need to? Split up the groups and cascade. Involve colleagues, peers, other managers of the organisation to build dialogue forums with smaller numbers, in workshops, for example.

The effectiveness of warm, personal communication is so superior that these efforts will be honoured. Just think of yourself: how much more involved would you feel after a small meeting with the CEO attended by you and a handful of colleagues instead of being one of 200 persons sitting on a chair in a town hall?

Now, this is a challenge for leaders of big organisations. But it can be handled – with a mix of warm and cold communication.

On true listening

My team at Allianz organised a wonderful semi-private farewell party for me in 2015, a couple of weeks after the official farewell reception. It was very touching. I was quite tired since my wife had to attend another event and I had my three-year-old son with me, who had enjoyed being spoilt by my former colleagues but was definitely ready for a well-deserved sleep. I said goodbye to the guests and shook hands with Jutta, a very important staff member whom I had worked with very closely and who was the perfect balance to my tempered leadership. A very quiet lady with a pretty narrow emotional volatility bandwidth, very reflective and with superb judgement, but also very thrifty with words. She just looked at me and her face started beaming, with a blissful smile, one notch above the Mona Lisa. She nodded slightly. I just took it as a message of gratitude for all the good and bad times we had worked together, solving some delicate questions by complementing our different approaches and characters. And I said: 'It was good working with you. Thank you.' And she kept on smiling and we parted.

The day after we had to speak about a very interesting job move she had been offered within the company. I was acting as sparring

▶

partner before she met Xavier, the local CEO for their final discussion for the new job. I recommended she consider that the CEO and she spoke two different languages. Jutta's language is the language of rationality, of a job description, of clear goals and KPIs and of sound expectation management. I knew her very well and I knew she would base her decision and her questioning of the CEO on what was expected of her and how one would measure her success. But I also knew Xavier very well and he is a leader who appreciates personal and corporate loyalty, he is used to working with 'buddies' and he actually had used this term twice in my conversation with him on Jutta. He said: 'I think Jutta can become my buddy and she would become part of the leading team, the buddies I want to manage this subsidiary with.' So, I suggested to Jutta that she might find a compromise in her discussion with the CEO, between her quest for the precise job framework and Xavier's need for a reassurance on her trustworthiness as a loyal member of the top-team. I told Jutta: 'You see, people speak different languages. You are not a wordy person and you very rarely express any emotions with words. But yesterday, for example, when we said goodbye at my farewell party, I interpreted your facial expression as a sign of gratitude for our long cooperation. I may be wrong, but I feel that you express your emotions like this and not verbally ...'

There was silence. Then she cleared her throat and said: 'You were absolutely correct.' She paused and repeated: 'You are absolutely correct.'

People speak different languages and with a little mindfulness we can learn to listen to these different idioms and understand and respond to them.

Before we get deeper into the different dimensions of listening, let's pause for a second.

What are the most important practical goals of good listening for a Listening Leader, next to earning the name?

There are two. First, to learn. To truly understand. Managing the process of listening allows us to learn and integrate the input into action, or strategy. It enriches and improves the quality of the management action, makes it more sustainable, grounded on more solid pillars, a stool with an additional foot.

Second, to become aware of the importance of listening for the greater good of the company and of society with *accepted* market mechanisms. This may grant the company the license to operate – and therefore thrive.

The most important thing about listening is another, however: Good listening is a wonderful experience. If you are even only minimally interested in people, good listening will open doors, will establish trust, it will expand your knowledge and your feelings and can lead to pure bliss. But while this truly matters for our lives, it would be an unlikely reason for your boss to be happy hearing that you read this book. Unless your boss already *is* a Listening Leader.

Richard Sennett explains that good listening skills are about 'closely attending to and interpreting what others say, before responding, making sense of their gestures and silences as well as declarations.'[4] I like this definition – it's as good as it can get in one sentence.

The different dimensions of listening

We have many ways to express our thoughts and emotions, from speaking to grunting to rolling our eyes to angrily waving our arms to shouting to ... being quiet. And if all these efforts aren't to be in vain, we better swap position and rather than just sending these signals, we should start learning to read them. Learn to listen. The first thing you need to know about good listening is summed up wonderfully by Anne Scoular, the Southern Star of Business Coaching (she's from New Zealand, after all). Answering the question 'How do you listen better?' she answers: 'Step 1: stop talking!'[5]

Quiet, or the sounds of silence

When I was a young reporter, one of my mentors, a great journalist and an even better novel writer as well as a man of broad knowledge and deep wisdom, Franco Mimmi, taught me a powerful trick.

▶

I had told him how scared I was to interview experienced states-men, mature central bank governors, long-standing CEOs while I had barely started to shave every second day. He told me the story of the Greek philosopher Zeno, who said: 'The reason we have two ears and only one mouth is that we may hear more and speak less.' As practical advice for interviewing the alpha-wolves in politics and business he said: 'Use silence. Let them talk. Dare to pause. Don't be scared of the void. They will tell you everything.' He was so right.

What was only a *ruse* to get my journalistic story later turned out to be a powerful means to truly learn from the other. To allow for a true sharing of knowledge, of emotions, of experience. The tool remains the same. The purpose is different from the journalistic one, slightly on the verge of being a trap for the speaker. Instead of simply becoming a trap, the higher value of silence is to lead to the contrary, to building trust. So practise it. As short as your tongue may be, you will technically be able to bite bits off the tip enough times to learn the lesson. Quiet will not let you down. Or, as Nancy Kline puts it: 'Consider how long you think you could bear to be quiet and let someone think out loud. With only the occasional benign murmuring and nod and smile of under-standing from you and the occasional question requesting even more thoughts, a person in your presence might just turn into a genius – at least, for that moment.'[6]

Do not interrupt

Chatty cultures such as the Italian allow for frequent interruptions in conversations. When Irish men sit in a pub the different layers of a conversation are like a complex cobweb that everybody weaves, still able to follow somewhat of a red thread. As the poet and good friend James McCabe, an Irishman living in Germany, once acutely observed about Germans in a pub: 'They may be drunk like pirates after a bounty but they will wait until Otto has finished to lull his sentence before Franz burps out his wisdom. Everybody will listen to Franz before Fritz will share his fundamental views on that questionable penalty in the last football derby.' This is something peculiar about the German language where the verb comes last in – sometimes enormously long – sentences. So, if you want to know whether the protagonist of a story told in German has died or survived you literally have to wait until the last word of the story. This is how I, an extroverted Italian boy moved to Germany, learned to listen. It suddenly convinced me that not interrupting wasn't such a bad thing in other languages, too. Interrupting is rude, of course, but it mainly is stupid. Because only a conversation where everybody has the opportunity to fully vent their thoughts with no interruption is a respectful conversation. Respect allows for the unthinkable to be expressed, without fear of derision. It will allow that one single contribution to emerge that will change the whole game in your business.

Proper feedback

If you want to know what feedback is useful for, play a round of Chinese Whispers with your team. The rules of the game are simple. You are only allowed to repeat to the neighbour on your right what you heard from the neighbour on your left. You have only one chance to say what you heard. No discussion is allowed. You start by whispering a couple of words into the ear of the first team member and this goes on until the words have reached the last team member who is then allowed to loudly repeat the words. I play this regularly with my students and the results are appalling. You start with the gentle words 'nice lady' and you end up with the serial killer's confession 'sliced baby'. How come? Because the rules of the game cut out the feedback, that wonderful mechanism by which we check that we have heard what was said.

Feedback is not forced upon anyone if it is to be effective. It may be offered but it has to be wilfully and consciously wanted by the recipient. If someone is not interested in your feedback you may as well keep it to yourself. And if you want to grow, ask for feedback.

Feedback has to be specific and focused on a behaviour, an event, or on something that has been said. It is not a judgement of a person, rather it is a reaction to a singular thing.

If you want this feedback to be heard, it's advisable to keep the ratio of positive and negative feedback to three positives for each negative.[7]

What is a bad listener?

Danuta is an incredibly intelligent equity partner at a management consultancy in Poland. While she successfully managed one key client, she couldn't figure out why she wasn't able to win new business with new clients, despite having a compelling corporate proposal. I was also perplexed. Danuta had been very engaging in our delightful first meeting. She had told me about her interesting life and career and what she wanted to achieve. However, once we started our coaching, it became clear that Danuta didn't listen. She was talking *at* potential new clients, telling them all about herself and her company but it was all one-way traffic. She didn't ask these potential clients about themselves and their business, their challenges, desires and needs. She was too busy talking to listen, find out and then think how she could help. Once she'd finished talking to me, I started to ask her a question and she interrupted halfway through, assuming she knew what I was going to say. She didn't. And she was too busy talking over me – answering a question I hadn't asked – to notice. So once she'd finished speaking, I tried again. And it happened again. I began to understand how her potential clients must have felt. And as her coach, I could give her honest feedback of how I was experiencing her and how others might be too. This wasn't the way to build rapport, trust and great professional relationships. Listening is.

The 'active listening' trap

Beware of cheap shortcuts. There are a lot of good pieces of advice you can find on listening: nod frequently; sum up what the other person said, paraphrasing it, showing that you listened and understood; show interest with your full body – don't lean back, don't put your feet on the table (yes, I read that advice and it was not in a survival guide for jail or a manual for opium caves). They sometimes come under 'active listening'. Nothing wrong with it except for the bitter taste in my mouth that they are 'tricks' to *pretend* to listen. From good coaching practice we know, for example, that paraphrasing is not necessarily the best thing to do: if someone uses one specific word, she means that word and not a synonym. Paraphrasing then only shows that you can find other words for a term. A good skill, but not evidence for good listening. Just imagine talking to your boss and he practises *all* of those 'active listening' tricks. Wouldn't you probably notice and find this to be highly annoying because it feels instrumental, mechanical, schemed, not sincere?

As always, there are no absolutes.

If there is really no listening culture or if Mr Talkative suddenly applies one of these techniques, it might turn into a useful exercise, as artificially as it may have been performed.

The listening monster

I once almost craved to disappear into the carpet of a boardroom by a sense of shame never experienced before. It was after a tough preparatory session with Tony, an enormously assertive manager with a consultant background. Great in most disciplines, but definitely not in listening. Now he had been promoted to a top position and he needed to lead a very senior team whose support he depended upon. We discussed the importance of listening and he made pages of notes, asked many questions and seemed to have grasped the gist of why listening would help him grow in the organisation. The next day he had his first meeting with the top team. Igor was asked to inform everyone on the latest developments in an important market. The operations were loss making and the grapevine had already given up on Igor, thinking him likely to be fired, in spite of being the big CEO's darling. Igor starts to give his update. And Tony suddenly, and, at least to my observation, abruptly turns his chair towards Igor, throws his right elbow onto his knee and leans his head on his fist intensely looking Igor in the eyes. He seems to inhale every word Igor spells out, he nods vigorously, smiles profusely at Igor and the more he applies the lessons of the previous day the more I sweat blood. I'm really embarrassed. Tony's posture is so ridiculously exaggerated and artificial that not only Igor, the whole team simply must feel that Tony is only pretending to listen, an attitude even worse than distracted dozing. I knew I was responsible. I was Dr Frankenstein

▶

and I had created this Listening Monster, this Fake Listening Robot. It would turn into a disaster. I wanted to melt into oblivion. At some point the good Lord had mercy on all of us and the meeting ended. I tried to sneak out of the room when Igor came to me and asked if he could have a word. I knew my days were numbered. He would figure out that I was the cause of such a fake freak show and would bite my head off. But Igor beamed. 'Have you seen? Can you believe this? For the first time in my life I have seen Tony really listening!' What had happened was clear, at this point: Igor hadn't noticed the exaggeration, he simply experienced for the first time not being interrupted by Tony, not being corrected and flooded with the consultant jargon Tony normally used showing off his superior intelligence. It was such a novelty that Igor didn't perceive the clumsiness of the listening exercise. And no one else had, either. It did the trick.

Reading the speaker

Body language is an art in itself. There are entire books, some of them with very funny illustrations and photos, on body language. The funniest are the Italian ones. Few people know that less than 10 per cent of the people of the freshly united Kingdom of Italy in 1860 spoke Italian. Before 1860 there was no Italy as there were no Italians speaking one language. The people spoke Neapolitan, Venetian, Piedmontese, Sardinian, Sicilian and so on. And they could barely understand each other. To this day I wouldn't be able to understand one single sentence in Sardinian. On top of it, my home country had been a patchwork of city states, regions, dukedoms and kingdoms which had been governed by Arabs, Spaniards, Germans, Austrians and French rulers before becoming a nation-state. This explains why we Italians speak with our hands. It's to bridge the language gap with the authority, represented by foreign rulers. Or with our fellow countrymen speaking remote dialects and languages.

This early training in body language has made me aware of the many shades of non-verbal expression.

Having had to attend family ceremonies and events at a very early age – and not necessarily enjoying them – I once played a game with one of my siblings. We were simply speaking about football but our faces made expressions of awe, we put our hands in our face and into our hair, we gaped at each other and immediately people around us would stop to speak and look at us, their faces mirroring our own expressions of an impending catastrophe. We then laughed out loud and made fun of the uncles and aunts who were scared by our apparent tragedies. My ears still hurt from my father's slap. The exercise had been a success though. It taught me the power of body language.

Neurology's progress in the last decades has allowed us to better understand how to read facial expressions. If our eyes wander while we speak, it may show that we are trying to remember something (looking to the upper left) or that we are trying to imagine something out of the blue (eyes looking to the upper right), if they turn to the left we try to remember something we have heard, to the right if we try to construct a sound never heard before. If our eyes are pointing down to the left we are just asking ourselves something; if they are eyes pointing down to the right we are experiencing feelings. Entire books have been written on these subjects, all inspired by John Grinder and Richard Bandler, the founders of neuro-linguistic programming (NLP).

What is important for the Listening Leader is the awareness that we basically have three ways of thinking: the visual way, the auditory way and the feelings way. Most of us have a preference. We can either see a memory, we remember a scene, a picture of people sitting around a table, how they were dressed, whether it was a day with summer light or with a grey sky. Others may remember perfectly well the music the radio played on a certain day, the voice of the grandfather, the sound of pans and dishes in the kitchen while others again can tell you exactly how they felt on that day, whether they held the hand of their sister or whether coffee was served, freshly brewed with a mild aroma.

Knowing about these thinking patterns allows us to read the other much better, to ask different people different questions, eliciting the best expression of their thinking and thereby reaching a much higher level of listening sophistication. If you know what language they prefer you'll be able to allow them to express themselves in the most perfect way and you can get the most out of the other.[8]

If you want to know whether you are a good Listening Leader, a simple exercise will do. It comes from the Bible of Leadership of General Electric, later published for the benefit of a larger public under the wonderful title of *Love 'Em or Lose 'Em*. The exercise goes as follows: 'Stop now and write down three or four things you learned from your employees this week. It could be process improvement ideas they have, a customer (or family) challenge they face, or a team issue they struggle with. If you can't list three or four things you learned, you probably have not been listening carefully enough to your employees.'[9]

Good communication and its impact on business results

Managers have tasks to accomplish and they have to perform according to their targets. Depending on the company they work for and the job they have, reaching the objectives may be a constant challenge, often frustrating and for some, simply threatening. Why should someone under this pressure consider any additional efforts in better communication instead of 'just getting the job done'?

Because good communication allows you to get the job done *and* to increase the performance of the organisation, thus allowing you to over-deliver on your targets.

Bain & Company found out that the answer to a very simple question would allow a company to predict its profitable growth.[10]

The question is: 'Would you recommend us to a friend?' The customer rates his answer on a scale of 0 to 10. Those who answer 0–6 are detractors, 7 and 8 are neutral, 9 and 10 are promoters. So, you take the percentage of customers who are promoters and subtract the percentage who are detractors and you get the net promoter score (NPS). The top companies have an NPS between 50 and 80 per cent. Most average between 5 and 10 per cent.

Others again have a negative NPS, which means they lose customers every single day and cannot sustain growth even by aggressively buying new business, a rather expensive exercise. Many excellent companies are run using NPS as the key performance indicator for the stakeholder customer, from Allianz, Apple, Lego, Philips to Progressive and many more.

The system allows us to look at the whole value chain of a company and identify all the moments of truth, all the factors that have an influence on the willingness of a customer to recommend the company. The simple fact that an insurance agent takes a call while he is advising another client personally, will never allow him to score a 10, as good as his piece of advice was. Being interrupted by a phone call in the middle of a conversation about your old age provisions is highly irritating and this irritation will never be mended in the whole insurance relationship from underwriting to payment.

NPS analyses allow us to sustain an enthusiastic customer experience – for big business and small companies, in all industries, in retail as well as in business-to-business propositions. Enthusiastic customers and promoters speak about their experience and become contagious new business generators. Everybody would concede that this is a fair way to grow.

At Allianz we have found a strong correlation between good communication and profitable growth. To investigate further we have worked closely with Bain and the media analysis institute Media Tenor, to relate good internal and external communication and profitable growth.

While carrying out this project we found out that bad communication habits and low scores given by the employees to their managers were clearly measurable in the laggards, companies losing market share and reducing the sustainable profit pool. Good communication habits and an engaged workforce were clearly seen in the loyalty leaders, companies gaining market share and being more profitable than the market. More details can be found in Chapter 7.

Let's summarise: It's a smart business move to invest in better communication and learn to listen.

Let's now look at how good communication can help drive business results.

Communication allows us to know, understand and reflect upon stakeholder interests – and to take them into consideration for our decisions. Business success, broadly speaking, is the result of *striking the right balance* between the enthusiastic stakeholders ('Only the NPS 10 counts') and the company's interest in sustainable, profitable growth.

Why can't we simply go all the way and take the input of stakeholders at fair value and just do what they tell us to do?

To make a point, sometimes it's useful to stretch arguments, or to create hyperboles, exaggerations. So, let's imagine what it would mean to blindly follow the stakeholders' wishes and to do this. Let's take extremes, what I call the hyperboles of creating stakeholder enthusiasm.

What would make the individual stakeholder happy and the company bankrupt? A product for zero price with top-notch quality would enthuse the customers. Paying out the whole turnover of the company as dividend might please the investor. Paying 100 per cent taxes on profits would make the Chancellor of the Exchequer rejoice. And wouldn't the employees cheer at the announcement that everyone gets five times their present salary and has to work only five hours a week? Everybody would be happy – for a moment – and a moment later the company would be bankrupt.

And, for the sake of argument: What might make the company happy and still drive it to failure, as well? Never paying any dividend, angering the investors, charging high prices for low-quality products, driving customers away, excelling in tax avoidance or even tax sheltering, not really amusing the taxman and so on.

So, matching the best possible outcome for stakeholders with the best possible outcome for a company is the difficult trick. And this is only achievable if the whole organisation interacts smartly with stakeholders, considers their input, weighs it against the general good of the company and adapts the company's strategy and behaviour to what has been heard from stakeholders, thereby continuously reinventing itself. And explaining what it does, creating transparency. There will always be acceptance for a company making good profits if the stakeholders benefit from the company's deeds.

So, you need transparency (see Chapter 1) and you need to constantly communicate with your public.

How a company can make best use of stakeholder input

The power of senses is known to all of us, even to those who lack one or more.

The cultivated illiterate

I was on a safari recently and there were six of us sitting in the jeep, some with binoculars, some without. Two of us had a PhD, one had an MBA, two were renowned experts, the last an illiterate. It was a quiet morning, very early and the zebras were pasturing not far from a flock of gnus. We all screened the horizon for predators, the grass slowly waving from a light breeze. One of us looked towards a small group of antelopes on the left, who stopped grazing and looked to our right. This friend slowly lifted his head and smelled the air, felt where the wind was coming from. He turned further to the right and whispered 'lions'. The rest of us couldn't see anything. After some time each of us saw that imperceptible reddish-yellow spot under a bush a couple of hundred yards away. Lemeira, the illiterate, our Masai guide, had given us another listening lesson.

Hearing the weak signals of the market and the stakeholders is as important as drawing the right conclusions from an attentive antelope to the direction of the wind. The experience evaluates these facts and the conclusion is that there must be lions to the far right. Listening has become a necessary survival skill in modern economy.

Going on a safari may seem the easier exercise in terms of organising the private listening to the weak signals of the predators (just have a good local guide on board). What do you do in a company to build a listening organisation?

As well as the traditional listening tools of classical business administration (such as market research) and the modern ones (datamining) there are a couple of tools I consider superior because of their trustworthiness.

Ombudsman: The Swedish idea

The Swedish Parliament first instituted an ombudsman back in 1809 to guarantee the application of laws. Ombudsman means representative, proxy, attorney. In business it refers to independent people that oversee the fair application of rules, who guarantee the stakeholders about the proper steps being taken by the organisations they oversee.

Take an excellent and impeccable professional with a clean ethical track record, maybe a judge or a scholar, ideally with grey hair, and make her look at complaints with the eye of the objective observer. Let the ombudsman (who could well be a woman) get an opinion on the dilemmas between the company's and the customer's (or any other stakeholder's) position. Let her be the steward of rules and values.

Here, again, everything stands and falls with the (communicative) qualities of that person. Is it just a bureaucrat, simply looking at paragraphs and their honest implementation? She may well comply with her duties but she is not a Listening Leader, she is not truly communicating.

What does it take for her to step up? She has to listen beyond the rules. Is there a legitimate point in a complaint? Is there a formally correct but emotionally wrong procedure that can be considered fair but also belittles the stakeholder and therefore makes him a detractor of the company?

An ombudsman that looks behind, that questions and challenges, is a precious ombudsman to the organisation that employs him or her.

This can be ensured by having one or two meetings a year, where the ombudsman convenes the departments most concerned by the complaints and listens to their point of view, gathers an impression of the leadership quality deployed in that area. Is the manager defensive? Is she understanding? Does she come up with alternatives to handle processes?

Organisations can improve enormously thanks to a good ombudsman. That is, if both the organisation and the ombudsman listen carefully.

John Smith, board member

Are you just an interested reader, maybe a civil servant who has no professional interest in business and whose role in the economic environment is simply being a customer? Well, you may aspire to become a board member of a stock-listed company. No need to take an MBA or practice management. Just by having a bank account with, let's say, Commerzbank in Germany. Or simply by using software from Oracle. These companies are just two out of hundreds of companies who have established a customer advisory board.

It basically is a high-level sounding board, a focus group. These boards work well if the prerequisites of communicative leadership are applied:

1. Customer advisory boards should be made of *up to 12 customers*. Some companies have bigger boards, I would advise against: a trustful discussion is only possible in a group not larger than 12 people.

2. Discussions in such boards have to be *relevant* for all participants and focus on the experiences of customers with the company and the products of the company.

3. *Understand the business of your customers* and their real-life situations in using your products. This may allow you to change your products or discover new ones for new customer needs. That's why you should be very attentive to their issues.

4. *Your role as a company is to be there to listen.* Don't use it as a sales opportunity – this is a listening opportunity. The talk is the customer's one, not yours. Make sure at least 80 per cent of the air-time is taken over by the customers, not by the company.

5. Be prepared to *change* your products and services and even adapt your strategy if there is relevant input from your customer advisory board.

A customer board can be an excellent way to integrate the other listening activities and provide the company with a picture as full as possible on the customers' views. It is also the opportunity for John Smith to take an active role in the life of the company providing him with important goods. It involves the participants and engages them in real discussions, which results in a much deeper understanding of customers' opinions, compared to blogs, tweets and posts on social media. They allow discussion of the inputs coming from other sources and complete the picture.

ESG boards – an opportunity to overcome greenwashing

I know I'm biased, but every time I read the term corporate social responsibility (CSR) I become suspicious. Is somebody trying to put lipstick on a gorilla? Generally said, I'm even suspicious of simple donations by a company. If it's a stock-listed company I always ask myself: who's paying for this donation and who gets the benefit? Clearly the money of a public company comes from money not spent on salaries or lowering prices for customers or money from the shareholders. Is this money benefiting any stakeholder of the company or a group of people totally unrelated to the company until that moment? Is this money serving the vanity of a hired manager to shine in the public light? Remember, it's not his money, it's the company's money.

I admit that sometimes I take too radical a view, but I remember a very shrewd politician, the late multiple Italian Prime Minister Giulio Andreotti saying: 'Suspecting ulterior motives is a sin, but you're mostly right.' I felt that was a respectable view when your gut tells you something may be wrong. My time served as a journalist left me with a natural suspicion for greenwashing and whitewashing, when soothing PR messages of responsibility for the environment accidentally meet that same company's reproachable deeds in pollution.

On the other hand I know that well-practised CSR can be a very important factor for the engagement of the employees and a factor increasingly important for the recruitment of talents. It is one of the four pillars of stakeholder acceptance. A company that wants to retain its license to operate has to respond to the demands by society. It has to be an accepted and welcome corporate citizen.

Good CSR should be:

1. Explained by the company: what is the purpose, what is the strategy, what are the principles of CSR?

2. Linked to the core challenges of the company and its industry.

3. A further listening device: to listen to society, non-governmental organisations, neighbours, the public at large.

4. Eligible to generate output that will impact the strategy and the business practices of the company.

Best-in-class companies are those who say what they think, listen to what the stakeholders say and do what makes the best possible sense for the company and its stakeholders. In other words, where CSR helps changing the company and improves it.

This is why I like the opportunity Environmental Societal Governance (ESG) boards can give. Some companies have already established ESG boards. The idea being to establish a body with the following characteristics:

1. Representing the top managers responsible for the business, not (just) the corporate communications people.

2. The ESG board establishes the environmental, societal and governance principles that the company will adopt and makes them public.

3. These principles are binding for all business units of the company.

4. This board engages in a permanent dialogue with external and internal stakeholder groups in order to listen to their concerns, proposals, best practices followed by other corporations.

5. This board is empowered to drive business decisions (within the proper corporate governance), and feed the input of the stakeholders into the strategic process of the company.

6. Every year the work of the ESG board is made as transparent as possible (some conversations need to be kept private, sometimes, because the external partners want this, not the company). Changes in the strategy of the company coming from the ESG board's work have to be made transparent as well as any other impact the ESG dialogue has had on the company and its stakeholders.

An ESG board is a modern and efficient way to channel the very diverse impulses coming from society and to challenge the *status quo* of the company. It may be because of diversity-related issues, concerns for the remuneration of the management or the carbon footprint of the company. These concerns have changed in the past and will continue to change in the future. Only a dialogue with stakeholders allows you to listen into society and not rely solely on media or research – as important as these outlets are in order to grasp trends and fundamental changes in society that may affect the company.

The importance of integrated reporting and of putting your money where your mouth is

We have seen some examples of how to set up a stakeholder (listening) governance that basically allows three things:

1. To listen to the stakeholders and enter into a true dialogue

2. To be ready to use this input to change your strategy and business

3. By involving and empowering the stakeholders this dialogue allows the company to constantly earn a license to operate.

As outlined in Chapter 1, companies providing first-in-class information produce either an integrated report (*One Report* by Bob Eccles and Mike Krusz of Harvard mentioned in the previous chapter) or they at least publish their performance against the four stakeholders in different reports.

What really matters is the question of whether management compensation is linked to those stakeholder KPIs. The company is credible if as many people in the company are compensated according to the feedback of the stakeholders as condensed in a key performance indicator. That's not something I need to ask at a shareholder meeting. I want to read this on the company's website: how much of the top managers' compensation depends on customer enthusiasm, employee engagement, investors' return and societal acceptance?

So, where do I put the little parcel with the stakeholders' input every day?

What do we do with all the input by stakeholders? Is there an address where the parcel is to be delivered with the daily or weekly input by stakeholders? If you want to get into action mode and shape the change there are three natural recipients for your input in your company:

1. **Your own team:** The dialogue with stakeholders doesn't occur in a void, somewhere in the atmosphere, separated from your everyday work, or in some debating society or Viennese café. It's in the daily interactions with our business partners. It's in your team, then, that this input by stakeholders is analysed and used to constantly improve your performance. Use your normal interactions with your staff to address this listening exercise. Is there a presentation on a new project? It should start with an evaluation of the EMMA of stakeholders (see Introduction). Are you discussing the mid-year review with your direct report? Let her start with rendering what the biggest learnings by stakeholders were in the half-year and what she did with them. Get your people used to always putting themselves into the 'victim's shoes'. Discuss strategy regularly with them as you should do with your own boss. Where are we in reaching our objectives? How has the context changed? How can we change ourselves or the context in order to create enthusiasm in our stakeholders, so that they recommend us to friends and family? Never forget the ultimate goal, success and acceptance, which is to increase profitable growth by recommendations from our customers, increase our attractiveness as an employer by becoming a great place to work, grow our market cap because investors like to buy our shares as recommended by the over-performance, gain and retain the

license to operate by society, when citizens and institutions recommend us as exemplary responsible corporate citizens.

2. **All the others in the company:** Most important is the C-suite. Where that address is, you know. But it may not be the right protocol in your company. Normally the recipients for the input by stakeholders are known, though. In most companies data on customers is managed by the marketing department. Normally, input from investors is dealt with in the investor relations department and in the CFO office. Employee and applicant's input related to the company is usually processed in the human resources department. Societal issues may have Public Affairs, Governmental Relations (lobbying), ESG office, CSR, legal department as their natural haven. This is an old silo approach, though. More and more often this input is broadly shared within the whole company on corporate social networks, in team-rooms and so on. Beware: sometimes these electronic 'containers' are so fragmented that the big picture gets lost. If this is the case, address it in the company. The company has an interest to gather this input and should make it easy to find the proper address (Ombudsman, Corporate Communications, CEO office) where all this information can be sent.

3. **The report:** If your employer publishes an integrated report, it will address the performance of the company towards all four stakeholders, along clear KPIs, benchmarked against the competitors. The team compiling the report should be grateful for your input. It may be a fact, a figure, but it also may be a compelling story about an important failure from which you and your team have learnt, a complaint you managed successfully or unsuccessfully. Share your experience – it's an episode of a saga that should keep your stakeholders awake reading until the sun rises.

Things to remember from Chapter 2, Communication

1. Management today is mainly communication.
2. Communicating means listening and speaking.

▶

3. Stop talking, be quiet and listen.

4. Do not interrupt.

5. Try to privilege 'warm communication'.

6. Consider creating a customer advisory board.

7. Consider an ESG board.

A millennial's view on inter-generational differences in how we communicate and their impact on corporate culture

The concepts of effective communication are the same as they have always been – listening, using empathy, constructive criticism. The shape that effective communication has taken over time has changed significantly (see Figure 2.1) and is changing at an incredible pace now.

One of the big changes, which reflects a societal shift, is the rise of informality and the breakdown of hierarchical barriers. Not only is there a clearly declining use of the formal address, the German *Sie* and the Italian *Lei*, but the boundaries on what is acceptable to say to others are also coming down. Like it or not, this is a development that is here to stay and so we must all adapt. While it may raise issues around respect and hierarchy, the resulting authentic communication and open exchange between different seniority levels can greatly benefit companies. Needless to say, this exchange has to be actively encouraged by creating a safe and informal environment in which junior employees are exposed to senior managers and a conversation is encouraged. Many companies are enabling this through open-plan offices and company retreats, which are a good start. But if the company culture is one encouraging formal inhibition, none of these strategies succeed in their goal.

This mobile and flat hierarchy environment is one of the attractive features of start-ups for young people. Because of the enthusiasm for the product and common goal that transpires in them, employees feel actively involved in their success. The open

Figure 2.1 From physical to digital in 70 years – communication patterns

	MATURISTS (born before 1945)	**BABY BOOMERS** (1945-1960)	**GENERATION X** (1961-1980)	**GENERATION Y** (1981-1995)	**GENERATION Z** (born after 1995)
Context	World War and post-war experience of food rationing Men and women with clear and separated roles Patriarchal families Rock and pop music	Cold War Economic miracle Woodstock Family-orientated Rise of the teenager Apollo 8 and landing on the moon	End of Cold War Fall of Iron Curtain Introduction of the first PC Early mobile technology Rising levels of divorce	Global terrorism PlayStations Social media Wars in Iraq and Afghanistan Reality TV Google Earth	Economic crisis Globalisation Smartphones Climate debate and energy crisis Arab Spring Individuals become media outlets Big data
Aspiration	'My own house'	'A safe job'	'A better work–life balance'	'To be free and flexible'	'Seeking security and stability'
Attitude towards technology	Passive	Early information technology adopters	Digital immigrants	Digital natives	Dependent on connectedness and IT – limited grasp of alternatives
Attitude towards career	Life-long employment	Careers are shaped by employers	Increasing self-shaping of a career, less loyalty to employer than to own career	Connected work – [digital] jobs 'with' firms, not 'for'	'Spiders in the web' – commute between organisations and 'pop-up' business
Signature product	Car	TV	PC	Tablet/smartphone	Google glass, nano-computing, 3D printing, driverless cars
Communication media	Typed letter	Telephone	Email and text message	Text or social media	Hand-held (or wearable) communication devices
Communication preference	Face to face	Face to face integrated with telephone or email	Texting or email	Online and mobile	Mobile (especially visual and audio)
Preference when making financial decisions	Face-to-face communication	Face to face ideally, integrated with conference calls and online	Online – would prefer face to face, if it is a viable option	Face to face	Solutions will be digitally crowd-sourced

communication culture enables them to voice their opinions and shape the company. And isn't that what all companies want when they speak of engaging employees?

Start-ups cater for some millennial needs

You might think: But people who go into start-ups are fundamentally different to those going to work for established corporations. Not necessarily. Of course, whoever founds start-ups is bound to be entrepreneurial. But employees who join at a second stage are no more so than employees of bigger, older companies. Reasons for joining a start-up include the flexible career progression, rapid learning curve as well as a high number and range of responsibilities. Yet this is not a separate world to the corporate world. Employees of start-ups are not bound to stay there. They might very well enter the corporate world and it is this impact that deserves a closer look.

For many millennials entering the workforce today, working in a start-up is very likely to be one of the first work experiences. This means some of their expectations are shaped there. Since they tend to be comfortable in the dynamic environment of those companies, they will look for that in later employers. While bigger companies can offer certain things these smaller ones cannot, such as formal training, a better salary and benefits package or a larger visibility and prestige, they often fail to offer the very characteristics millennials crave the most, especially when they have had a taste of it somewhere else: a sense of community and a platform for cross-sectorial, cross-hierarchical and cross-departmental communication.

Millennial coach and TEDxter Patrick Boland enlightened me to the statistic that by 2025, 75 per cent of the global workforce will be composed of millennials.[11] So if big companies want to still be relevant or even active, they should adapt to this generation's needs and preferences.

Increasing warmth of digital communication: social media

Now let's take a look at how millennials communicate. You might be tired of hearing about social media, but unfortunately or fortunately, they are here to stay. Actually, the drive behind them is here to stay. As we know, technology is moving incredibly fast, so social media might just be one of the major manifestations of these drives and new ones will follow.

More conventionally, communication which occurs through technology is of a colder nature, as explained in this chapter. The way in which millennials (and even more so, the Generation Z) use social media, however, might well be a way to make non-physical communication warmer. Through them, a more rounded set of interpersonal communication characteristics can be used, from voices, face expressions, body language, arguably even emoticons, memes and gifs to music, links and shares. While never an alternative for face-to-face communication with regards to the many impactful subtleties there involved, they could, if used in a certain way, make the nowadays necessary virtual exchanges warmer and therefore better.

Enterprise social networks

What happens when social media meet the work environment? They can give a new dimension to intra-organisational communication. But an enterprise social network left alone cannot do all the work. No matter how well equipped with features, if not used correctly and with the right spirit, it is of no value to a business. It needs to be used as an enhancer of communication and driven by a company culture thriving for connectivity. Employees of older generations should not be left out. Millennials can drive the initial take-up, lead by example and so show and teach other employees what can be achieved with these media. One of the most wonderful outcomes of a successful implementation is a more widely shared knowledge across the company. Now, with the help of tags and search function, I might find out that a team on the other side of the world is interested in the same topic as my team for a different project. Maybe they can teach me something they have learned working on it, or maybe we can share the workload. What results is the breaking down of silos, which is such an important element of the current and future successful company.

Social media for improved customer service

Another way in which social media impact the business world is in the realm of customer service. We, as customers, want companies to listen to us, to our ideals, ideas and comments. In some industries and smaller companies, my comment might reach the higher ranks of leadership. Traditionally, that's where a reaction can occur and subsequent change can happen. Just like when you tell a waiter to call the manager to complain about something, or the chef to compliment a dish, social media are our vehicle to reach the leaders and be heard. And the great thing is that leadership within customer service is now increasingly being shared throughout the hierarchical ranks of companies. These media can be a vehicle for employees to become ambassadors of the brand, to listen, to respond. One example is Dutch airline KLM's response to the challenge of the Iceland volcanic ashes crisis in 2009. A little while before social media customer service became the norm, KLM, overwhelmed by calls and emails by angry customers stranded all over Europe, set up a social media room to answer to the complaints and frustrations which were being aired on there in a matter of hours. Fuelled by the common goal of providing good service to their customers, KLM employees volunteered to help answer the comments day and night throughout this crisis. Instead of waiting for hours on hold to be able to speak to an operator, customers were able to receive a response to their queries much quicker. This was a successful mitigation of a potential customer dissatisfaction catastrophe. Now most companies have social media departments, and some, including Nestlé, Cisco and Mastercard, even have a social media listening room.

Let's open our approach to how communication occurs within business, invite in the informal format adopted by innovative company cultures and discover how it can be enriching. Then let's re-evaluate our current channels and habits of interaction: what to keep, what to adapt and what to toss.

Chapter

3

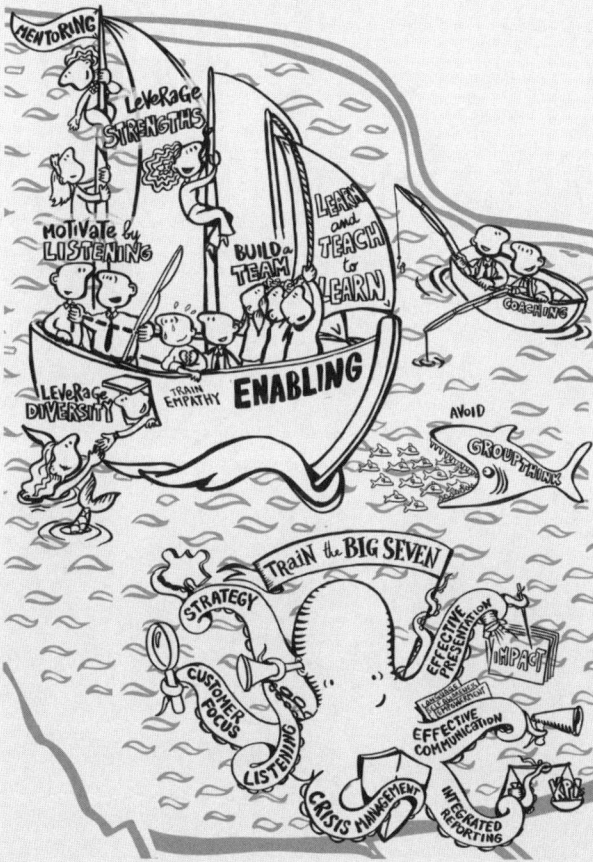

Enabling: How to increase your own and your employees' performance by learning and teaching to learn

- How and when leaders can enable themselves
- Why leveraging strengths is better than mending weaknesses
- An overview of how good learning improves communicative leadership.

The flaws of a genius

Imagine the following situation: Albert works for you and you start the yearly performance review. His haircut is not what you would expect from a corporate soldier. He cracks wildly politically incorrect jokes and in meetings he tends to ramble. He posted a picture of himself on the company's social network where he sticks out his tongue until it almost reaches his chin. This does not fit with your company's desired behaviour and you go through the corporate template with him and address all these weaknesses and demand a change in looks and behaviour if he wants to reach his targets. He mumbles something about some major breakthrough that he is working on that will change the world. You cut him off, you don't have much time for his dreams and you give him a clear deadline until when he has to show he got the message. Next thing you do (is he still in the room?) you fill in the empty boxes on your computer. Name: Albert. Surname: Einstein. Date of birth and so on. Then you hear him (he's still sitting there!) saying: 'I quit.' You have just lost a genius in your team, in the wake of finding the relativity theory ...

Absolutely crazy, this example, isn't it? Well, not so much. For more than a hundred years the best human resources practices – and management practices at large – have been heavily influenced by psychoanalysis, the science of trauma, or problems. This generated corporate functions focusing on the simple (actually, simplistic is the right term) assumption that humans are full of weaknesses to be corrected. Knowledge, behaviour and social skills are supposed to be described in a uniformed way throughout the organisation and every individual has to reach those standards by improving in the areas he's weak, mercifully termed 'areas of development' of what in HR jargon are called the organisation's 'capabilities'. And most of the time devoted to training and all other forms of corporate education are invested in addressing those weaknesses focusing on the 'untidy appearance and him poking out his tongue' instead of leveraging on the strengths.

While it is totally legitimate that an organisation seeks a common denominator of its staff in terms of qualifications and desired attitudes and behaviours, it is simply a waste of huge potential if one stops at this and doesn't go one step further. And I obviously don't mean the step of our imaginary example, to let Dr Einstein attend seminars on the proper outfit, haircut or social demeanour. I mean tapping the potential of every individual to make his or her skillset contribute to the organisation's well-being in the most effective way. This starts by listening. Understanding the strengths, talents and skills of the individuals allows us to reach out to these people, to what truly motivates them and only then one can see – together with the individual and by initiative of the staff member – how to best enable this person to grow, deploy their potential and meet the organisation's demands. The role of the Listening Leader is to make two lines converge: the line of the individual's skills and the line of the skills demanded by the organisation in order to thrive.

Enabled managers and employees can translate the strategy of the company into their daily working context, if they understand the strategy. Better, if they also shaped the strategy because the top management listened to their input creating it. But the biggest value of enabled people in the workplace is their constant ability to adapt to changing situations in the working environment and translate these changes into different behaviours, improving processes, or, in other words, a better company.

Enabling people doesn't mean giving them files from A–Z that they can look up when faced with a certain situation. This reminds me of a funny situation within a pretty serious context.

A manual for all events? No way

One day Alfred, the head of our Hamburg branch, called me and – in between coughs of heavy laughing – told me he was in the middle of a crisis. As head of the company's global crisis team I was all ears. A guy laughing out loud and having a crisis means either he is in severe shock (why would he be laughing during a crisis, otherwise?) or that the crisis isn't so big after all. Well, never judge. I was wrong in my assumptions.

What had happened? We had an insurance client with disposophobia, or compulsive hoarding. This person not only had an apartment full of newspapers, pizza boxes and unopened letters, he was also a chain-smoker. His stumps didn't always land in ashtrays and sometimes they were still lit. Not surprisingly his apartment caught fire. We, his insurance company, decided not to pay the full amount of the claim because of his gross negligence. These things are unpleasant, but they happen.

What was unusual was that this man went into a shop for special materials and bought industrial glue, a chemical to fix bricks and stones, stronger than anything normal people normally use. He found an interesting way to put the glue to work. He spread it on his hands and glued himself to the glass window of the entry hall of our building. The head of our branch office had called me when the street in front of our building was already crammed with ambulances, the press with cameras, hundreds of curious passersby and our client was shouting: 'Give me my money!' Now, why was Alfred laughing? Because two minutes before calling me, the head of our security team stormed his office waving our crisis manual and cursing this 'damned, useless Italian'. He meant me, the head of the crisis team, responsible for the publication and the content of the crisis handbook. And he explained why: 'Look at this useless manual! How should I handle this situation? Read it! Tell me if you can find "glue" under "G"!'

In today's volatile world you cannot foresee every crisis. There can't be manuals with all possible scenarios from A to Z. In most cases people in distress wouldn't even know where to look for the manual. An enabled person would know what general rules to apply to a crisis. One of them is to use common sense. And common sense suggested that the first thing to do was to consult the best possible doctors to make sure one could detach our customer from the glass wall with the least possible damage to his health, including cutting out the glass where his hands were glued on and bring him to a hospital with two glass circles around his hands for the surgeons to do the rest.

This taught me an important lesson. Never again would I do crisis training without stressing how much common sense matters. Much better to teach and train principles instead of lulling our own people into security with a manual that simply cannot answer all the questions. So we changed our crisis training from single scenarios to a broader picture addressing principles in order to be able to tackle also incredible scenarios. Alfred's experience with our disposophobic client delivered the perfect story to be told to make this point.

The Listening Leader understands that enabling his people is a big leap towards his own freedom from being called day and night to address issues not foreseen in working manuals.

We owe the understanding of the potential of humans to the enormous progress of psychology in the last two decades. The birth of positive psychology, fathered by Martin Seligman and Mihaly Csikszentmihalyi, allowed us to address peak performance and optimal human functioning.

Enabling starts at home

Knowing where your strengths are and how to build on them through proper training, coaching, mentoring and learning at large starts with yourself. Whatever is being described in this and the next chapter always applies to you and your team. You have to walk the talk. It's in your own interest. Not only will the team follow more easily if they see that you lead by example, you allow yourself to perform better by investing into your own knowledge.

Why should I bother?

Oh my god, training again … I see the CEO skipping that chapter once the word 'training' is mentioned. 'So much money is spent on training and the staff is still not up to my intelligence …'. You may be right that lots of money is spent on training. But first check how much is invested in training to teach Albert Einstein what 'look' he should have and how to mend his 'weaknesses'. That's a great budget item where you can save money. Not all of it is really necessary.

Then you might want to ask yourself whether attracting talents is something you want or whether you prefer to get the scum of the labour market. It may be a smart choice if you run a mob in your neighbourhood, but not if you want to turn a legitimate business into success.

For the talents of the Y generation constant learning and training is a make or break question: you offer it and they might join, you don't and they won't. If you neglect this aspect, if enabling is not part of your philosophy and of your practical toolbox, you can forget about being able to attract young talents. So, addressing enabling properly is a must. Since you hold this book in your hand anyway, you might consider continuing the reading. Well, not if you want to hire only those who adore being squeezed like lemons, working late hours, having no private life, the health of a young lion and adore living from the knowledge they got in business school ages ago. It still might become quite a costly exercise to only go for the masochists. If they are high performers, you already have to compete for them with investment banks and corporate law firms, excellent biotopes for these work-horses who happen to be rather expensive.

How to identify strengths and build on them

In recent years positive psychology and legions of academic researchers have provided us with excellent tools to assess one's strength. At the beginning of the enabling journey stands the awareness of one's strengths. For a person totally happy with her job, it might be interesting to see how one can improve her performance by leveraging her strengths. For someone thinking about a new career, rather than asking whether we have the right strengths for our present job we should check what the right jobs are for our talents. In all cases it is useful to become better aware of who we are as professionals. What positive psychology tells us is that happiness and fulfilment can be influenced by leveraging our own strengths. The role of the Listening Leader is to unleash this potential. To do this, knowing about our staff's and our own strengths is tantamount.

Should you think that's a nice-to-have, beware (unless you don't care about increasing your own performance and that of your team). This book is about increasing performance in a natural way, using conventional wisdom. Common sense tells us that we should be mindful of solid evidence. If the emphasis of the performance reviews with your staff is on your team members' performance strengths this will drive performance by 36 per cent, almost 60 per cent higher than focusing on performance weaknesses, which can cause almost 27 per cent decline in employee performance. What about gaining more than 50 per cent better performance compared to peers that don't get it? Maybe this competitive angle does the trick to tip you in the right direction.

You can find the most common and useful ones in the 'Tools' box at the end of this chapter.

Before that I'll explain that enabling starts by understanding strengths and motivations of the individuals, leveraging the potentials of teams, learning and teaching to learn, increasing empathy and tapping into academic research.

On motivation

Why is motivation actually so important? The Neapolitan in me says: it allows the deployment of energies *I* don't have to come up with. It allows me to lead a better life as a leader, because motivation holds all the ingredients to allow people in your team to be much more self-directed, autonomous and engaged than when there is no motivation. There will be a lot fewer monkeys in your professional life (read more on monkey management in Chapter 4 on 'Empowerment'). But it's not only lessening your burdens. It drives performance, it reduces attrition, it thereby saves you costs of recruiting, onboarding and training those new hires you would need to replace your best people who leave your team, because of lack of motivation.

Motivation is a powerful driver of performance; it's the glue that keeps your team together in difficult times and creates an environment of creativity and energy. Plus, it is more fun working with motivated people.

An array of different theories and subsequent research has attempted to find answers to the question of what motivates people. As Daniel Pink brilliantly summarises in his book *Drive: The Surprising Truth About What Motivates Us*,[1] beyond the basic monetary compensation allowing us to live our lives, three things motivate us: *autonomy, mastery* and *purpose*.

Autonomy, having control over one's own actions, is the key to engagement in the workplace. At a basic level, the sense of freedom carries a different, more internalised sense of responsibility, which fuels one's drive to achievement more than when control is exerted from an external source. On top of that, it opens the door to creativity and innovation, which are stifled by constricted and dictated working conditions.

Second, the goal of learning and finally **mastering** something, be it playing an instrument or coding, is powerful in directing energy towards a task. During Clementina's organisational psychology studies, a professor introduced her to the findings that a mastery orientation in students consistently produced better grades than a performance orientation, generating a nice and nerdy little 'inception' effect. In a work context, approaching work with the goal of successfully completing a project is not as powerful a predictor of success as wanting to learn all about it and being able to be an expert in this particular topic.

Finally, **purpose** rounds up the elements making up intrinsic motivation. It seems intuitive that any work to be done needs to serve a purpose. Why else would it need to be done? However, in the reality of day-to-day life, the purpose is often removed from the work we do, as we go about our tasks without thinking of what purpose they serve. But how much verve are we putting into those tasks compared to those we clearly see and support the meaning of? The answer is obvious.

Basically we are motivated by fulfilling our expectations and the meaning we find in our job, by recognition of our skills as well as what we master and by freedom of choice in our working life.

You won't find this information about your staff on their CVs. Not only because bios are still mainly compiled according to standard templates that focus on education and working experience, but also because very often people actually aren't necessarily aware of what truly motivates them unless they experience it. Motivational drive can also change during one's life.

Another good reason to listen.

When you recruit you can ask people what truly motivates them. When you are being recruited and meet people from the prospective employer you can ask them about their motivation. Generally speaking, if you are aware of the people around you, you are already starting on the right foot. Every performance review is a wonderful opportunity to discuss motivation.

Recognition and appreciation are very powerful drivers of motivation. So, when you discuss, make sure you identify the kind of appreciation your colleagues are seeking. Not everyone loves to be praised in front of others. And most hate general words of gratitude, people want specific appreciation. Gary Chapman and Paul White have identified five languages of appreciation: words of affirmation, quality time with your people, acts of service to support them, tangible gifts and physical touch. They also have a test to figure out your own and other people's language of appreciation and its different dialects. This is a tool to boost the encouragement of people. Make use of it. It doesn't cost a dime and it pays off in retaining your best people.[2]

But why would you bother about what motivates your people? They get a salary to do their job, they normally have performance indicators to measure their impact on the company and their team … 'You, as a manager, have more power and influence over the engagement and retention of your people than anyone else', as Beverly Kaye and Sharon Jordan-Evans put it, the authors of the brilliant guide to retaining good people, *Love 'Em or Lose 'Em*.[3]

The simpler answer on why you should bother is that you will lose one out of every two of your staff members if you are a bad boss. And guess who will be leaving? Those who are qualified and good enough to get a job somewhere else. 'A Gallup study of 7,272 US adults revealed that one in two had left their job to get away from their manager and improve their overall life at some point in their career.'[4]

Let me close this section with a small piece of advice that may open a door to superior performance: why don't you ask your single team members how they perform best? What does it take to increase your performance? Listen to their answer – you might be given the key to this person's performance potential.

Motivated through listening

Frank is an achiever. His over-performance was one of the few predictable variables in my team for quite some time when, more casually than not, in a conversation where I asked him how he was doing and asked the question twice, with a pause, letting him understand that I was truly interested, he told me he was very concerned about his partner Sven who was diagnosed with cancer. Sven had no family left except for Frank and Frank had already gone above and beyond just to be able to be close to Sven and still keep his job. I offered him a sabbatical to be able to care for Sven during his chemotherapy. Our HR department was cooperative: we could settle on a contractual solution that would leave Frank not only with the regular payment of his insurance, health, unemployment, and so on but also with his basic salary, without the variable compensation for the six months of this sabbatical. This allowed him to continue to have an income without needing to be in the office. I decided to appoint a young talent, Sarah, to take over Frank's job during his absence. It was clear to Sarah that this was a great opportunity, since she was too junior to be promoted to this job for the next two or three years to come. But she could practise and one of my most senior people volunteered to mentor her. Actually, Frank offered to regularly discuss job matters with Sarah whenever she needed to. She first hesitated, but when she saw that Frank was not at all disturbed, she took advantage of this offer. Frank felt he was still in the loop and was happy to share his experience with Sarah. When he came back to his

▶

job, he took over again and Sarah returned to her old job – for a year. Because she had shown great savviness in her interim appointment we were able to speed up her career progression. Both Frank and Sarah benefited from an opportunity arising from unfortunate circumstances. If one takes into account the sums paid for the two salaries in the six months of Frank's absence, both Frank and Sarah got less money: Frank because he didn't get the variable compensation in exchange for caring for his partner; Sarah didn't get a higher salary in spite of the six months in a more senior position. She did so for the purpose of gathering more experience. Both came out of this period more motivated and stronger. Sarah sped up her career progression and Frank put even more energy into his job once Sven had recovered. With cancer, one never knows. But so far, Sven is doing fine and that adds the decisive positive flavour to this story of small compromises for a greater good. The happy number cruncher would say: good overall performance for less money. Without this opportunity, you probably would have lost Sarah. Challenging her allowed you to motivate and keep her. You saved money to recruit, get onboard and train a successor for Sarah. That alone can easily be an additional year's salary. Cynical remark, but right. Proving the point that motivation doesn't come from money but from being listened to, deeply. Which, in turn, can bring financial benefits.

Building teams and creating a high-performance organisation

Most of what you have read so far deals with individuals in an organisation, the leader and the single employee. We all know, however, that most of the performance is delivered by the sum of individuals, if they work as a team. Intuitively we assume that more brains together deliver more output than one single brain, as developed as it might be. But this is not always the case. To be able to tap into this potential, the interaction between these brains has to be effective. We all know that groups of people can take wrong decisions just because they act as groups, maybe following the leader on a wrong track without the ability or will or permission to voice objections in time. Managing teams isn't as trivial as putting many intelligent people in one room and ordering 'Now, perform!'

There is not much good literature on how to create high-performance teams. But sometimes you don't need much literature; just the right one. This is what Jon Katzenbach, a McKinsey director, and Douglas Smith, a consultant, achieved with their book *Wisdom of Teams*.[5] They advise addressing six basic issues to make teams perform:

1. Don't create big teams, *keep small numbers*. As a rule of thumb, teams should consist of less than 20 people. My own experience is: 12 is the magic maximum number for a team to build trust and perform (see Chapter 2).

2. *Gather complementary skills.* The component of the good teams should contribute with a mix of technical or functional expertise in the matter of teamwork. In other words, they should be competent. Then, they should be good at analysing issues, problem solving and decision making. Lastly, the team members should have interpersonal skills from listening to risk taking, helpful criticism support and objectivity, among others.

3. The team must have a clear and meaningful *purpose*. This should be discussed, refined and shared by all team members. And it should matter to the whole organisation, well beyond the team per se.

4. Have *specific* performance *goals*. The objectives of the teamwork should be measurable, the product of the team should be defined clearly and it should deliver things to the organisation that single individuals do not already contribute.

5. Committed to a *common approach*. Katzenbach and Smith found out that the 'how' of the teamwork matters for performance more than normally assumed. Before engaging in the task of the teamwork the team should spend some time in crafting a common working approach addressing the economic challenge, the administrative aspect and, last but not least, the social aspect of interaction.

6. The team has to have a sense of *mutual accountability*. This point addresses the sense of responsibility of the individuals working in a team. If the team manages to build trust between the members and a strong commitment to the common

purpose they will succeed in building a mutual sense of accountability for the product of the team work.[6]

Teamwork is becoming more and more important. Tapping the potentials of the skills and minds in an organisation and putting them at the service of the strategy involves more and more tasks being addressed in teamwork, across organisational siloes, including diverse skills and personalities.

Teamwork doesn't stop in front of the C-suite, actually that's where good team work starts.

Well, where it *should* start. Because the reality is: the C-suite generally lags behind the learning efforts by rank and file in spite of all the big words on lifelong learning, the need to change and adapt to change and all the nice things that you might hear from the very same people who preach water and drink wine. No, the track record of top managers undergoing life-long training is not excellent. Just ask the best business schools in the world how big their population of students is in executive programmes designated to CEOs or other C-suite members.

Should you be interviewed by a C-suite member for a job you've applied for, just ask when their last learning, training, coaching occurred and listen carefully. If they don't come up with good answers, you can still go for this job. But don't complain afterwards, when your needs for development are not being addressed. You knew before, when you got the wobbly answer by the Big C-guy. That company doesn't have a leadership that leads by example.

How to avoid bad decisions in groups by good listening and more

Sometimes, one can be baffled at how naïvely top management goes about its own procedures and how poor decision-making processes are. Ask a board member of a company along which formal and informal rules their board is organised. Is it proper to voice a concern once all the other board members have supported a certain decision you think is plainly wrong? Is it good to find unanimity on an issue within three minutes?

Why should I bother at all with these questions?

Because otherwise a wrong decision might haunt you. Because you may have missed an important detail that changes the impact of a business plan. Simply because you would be a worse performing company because of your naivety or, worse, negligence.

Excellent research has been carried out on how to avoid 'group-think'[7] and thereby improve and optimise decision-making processes in groups, typically the C-suite. Here is the summary, as provided by the Meyler-Campbell Tutorial Resources for their Business Coach programme:

1. State the problem clearly, indicating its significance.

2. Break a complex problem into separate parts, and make a decision on each part.

3. Encourage each member of the group to evaluate their own and others' ideas openly and critically.

4. Be suspicious of unanimity, especially when arrived at quickly.

5. Ask influential members to adopt an external or critical 'devil's advocate' stance, or leave the group for periods.

6. Discuss plans with objective outsiders to get reactions.

7. Use expert advisers to design the decision-making process.

8. Avoid wide difference in status among members, or if present, adopt means to minimise them.

9. Develop agreed procedures in advance to deal with crises or emergency situations.

10. Consider external reactions to the decision, and explore several possible alternative scenarios for these.

11. Use sub-groups (committees) to develop alternative solutions.

12. Admit shortcomings (when 'groupthink' occurs, members feel very confident; admitting some flaws in argument might open them up to new ideas).

13. Ensure those entrusted with implementation understand exactly what they are to do.

14. Encourage the group to evaluate the skills within it, and find ways of improving them.

15. Have a last chance meeting, allowing people to voice any concerns before implementation.

Just think where Volkswagen would be, had they applied these principles. Had the significance of the issue (high standards for exhaust fumes in the United States) been stated clearly, had they encouraged each member of the group to voice a concern, had they used expert advisers, asked an objective outsider … but they didn't. And note points numbered 3, 6, 7 and 10: They are all items about good listening, about understanding the reasons of the involved stakeholders and adapting your strategy to it. The Listening Leader knows where the obstacles are and if she doesn't, she will be brave enough to ask and her team will have been encouraged to voice concerns and propose ideas to address the concerns.

Learn and teach to learn

The 70/20/10 rule

There is an ideal ratio on learning, based on evidence from practitioners. It is based on three types of experience: challenging *assignments* (70 per cent), developmental *relationships* (20 per cent) and coursework and *training* (10 per cent). Let me quote the Center for Creative Leadership (CCL) material on their important findings:

> The 70-20-10 rule emerged from 30 years of CCL's Lessons of Experience research, which explores how executives learn, grow and change over the course of their careers.

> 'The underlying assumption is that leadership is learned,' says CCL's Meena Surie Wilson. 'We believe that today, even more than before, a manager's ability and willingness to learn from experience is the foundation for leading with impact.'

The 70/20/10 rule seems simple, but you need to take it a step further.

All experiences are not created equal. Which experiences contribute the most to learning and growth? And what specific leadership lessons can be learned from each experience?

To help you (and your boss or direct reports) match your learning needs to the experiences most likely to provide that learning, CCL has researched and mapped out the links between experiences and lessons learned.

Five universally important sources of leadership learning stand out:

1. Bosses and superiors

2. Turnarounds

3. Increases in job scope

4. Horizontal moves

5. New initiatives.[8]

So, give learning a chance

Our brain is a powerful organ. How powerful it is has been researched for almost three centuries but only now are we starting to grab the enormous abilities hidden in our skulls. Once you start reading books on neurology and neuroplasticity you understand what they have that makes them superior to any thriller: those books are about how we can change our lives for the better by understanding how to use our mind. The best: it's not fiction, it's real. The key to happiness is within our heads, each of ours.

How esoteric. Do you think I'm crazy? And what does it matter to a manager who wants to become a leader? Let's put it in a nutshell: learning enables you and your people and makes you perform better. Does this sound more reasonable?

If the word 'training' smells too much of the schoolyard and classroom, try to call it learning or 'job enrichment', because that's what training leads to. 'Job enrichment means change in what your employees do (content) or how they do it (process).'[9]

The best training is that which involves the participants actively. Training not only has to enable people, it has to be done with enabling techniques themselves. The most important is participation. A colleague of mine always stressed he wanted to avoid 'Piz Buin trainings', referring to a wonderful mountain in the Alps, where people were lying in sun-chairs watching the peak and getting tanned. So, good training is not about sitting there and listening, but rather absorbing the knowledge by listening *and* responding.

Here are the three dimensions you need to cover for good training, and I'm referring to and summing up in my own words the experience of consultant Andrew Sobel.[10]

- **Principles.** Training on the principles of the organisation, the philosophy, stories that illustrate how these principles have been enacted.

- **Skills and behaviours.** You best train important skills and behaviours by role play, personal exercises, using case studies, videos and small group discussions. Interacting, observing and learning from the best.

- **Best practices.** Who's the best in an organisation at doing specific things? Learning benefits from observation and emulation and the discussion about them, the deeper understanding of excellent examples.

Well, if this sounds too generic, you may be right. The following paragraphs will be more specific. According to the 70/20/10 rule experience beats training 7:1. If I had to choose what to put into the 10 per cent box it would be what follows now.

Here is a list of what I consider the 'minimum package' of what a Listening Leader has to learn and constantly practise throughout her career. You could also say that what follows is the yearly programme of a corporate university. It's the training offered by the company to its employees in a company that practises or wants to practise communicative leadership. A company that wants to succeed sustainably needs to train all its employees in the following disciplines (see Figure 3.1).

The big seven to train repeatedly

1. **Strategy.** Every manager of an organisation has to update her knowledge on the company's strategy every year. Strategy is continuously adapted to the input from stakeholders and the market at large. So, a leader needs to not only personally convey stakeholders' input to the rest of the company and especially to the top management, she also has to be aware of the

Figure 3.1 Train the big seven – repeatedly!

1. Strategy:	Every employee should know what the strategy of the company is and how he/she contributes to the overall success.
2. Customer focus:	What are the drivers of customer enthusiasm? How can I/we contribute to creating this enthusiasm?
3. Listening:	How do I listen better? Whom do I share the input by stakeholders with?
4. Crisis management:	What am I supposed to do to *avoid* crises? What is my role in case of crisis, the dos and don'ts.
5. Effective communication:	How to establish a dialogue. How to train empathy, self awareness, language. How to address audiences. The importance of EMMA (Empathy Mentality Motivation Analysis).
6. Effective presentations:	Learn how to make your point, gather attention and have a real impact with your presentations. How to use presentations to gather feedback.
7. Integrated reporting:	Be aware of the overall performance of the company with respect to every single stakeholder; how good is it as an employer, providing services and products, growing the company value and behaving as a corporate citizen?

whole picture of the strategy and question it, understand it, be able to explain it to her staff and translate it into actionable items for her people and her area of responsibility. These actions have to be measurable in their effects on improving the organisation. In other words, every manager should be well aware of the key performance indicators. Every year, again.

2. **Customer focus.** Everybody in the organisation has to have a basic understanding of the customers of the company. How satisfied they are, what they complain about, whether they are enthusiastic about a product or service. They have to know where in the company the most customer-focused colleagues are from whom they can learn.

3. **Listening.** What motivates our stakeholders, the people and companies who interact with my department, whether they are colleagues or customers, investors, competitors, society at large? We can only learn that by listening. Listening can be learned and trained. How does one grab weak signals? How does one monitor the behaviour and the wishes of the stakeholders? How is big data applied within the company? Where

can one find data within the organisation? How can one convey complaints, whistleblowing, suggestions most effectively to the organisation? All these questions should be answered in modules accessible and complimentary for all managers of an organisation.

4. **Crisis management and crisis communication.** Learning how to best manage a crisis means learning how to avoid one. That's what listening (the previous point) can achieve. Should a crisis occur, however, it is absolutely necessary to have a crisis organisation which trains regularly and sharpens its skills with every training, paints constantly changing hypothetical crisis scenarios to be prepared to face them should they materialise. But what has to be taught to *all* managers and employees is not how the crisis organisation works but that there is one and how every employee should act if he thinks a crisis is about to occur, for example, whom to call, how to behave.

5. **Effective communication.** How does one convey information, how does one listen and respond, how does one interact with others? Effective communication is made of empathy, self-awareness, language, common sense. Every Listening Leader is a good communicator and this can be learnt. Every leader has to become a communicator and, finally, every employee has to, as well. Giving and receiving feedback is important for every learning organisation and every leadership situation. If you want to know what feedback is useful for, play a round of Chinese Whispers with your team.

6. **Effective presentations.** How often is a good cause spoilt by a bad presentation? Most PowerPoint presentations have little power and almost no point. Learn how to make your point and convey it with the power that leads to contagion, motivation, delegation and implementation. Don't forget most Roman emperors in their youth underwent a thorough education in rhetoric, an important branch of philosophy.

7. **Integrated reporting.** How did my company perform according to the main indicators? How do our customers, investors, employees, governments, supervisors and regulators, the media and relevant NGOs value our performance? Are they enthusiastic or infuriated and what about all those in between these extremes? Not knowing the basic financials killed the careers

of some managers I've met in my working life. But the Listening Leader needs to be fully aware not just of the financial KPIs but of all the others, too. This is also why I advocate a very simple KPI framework, limited to four KPIs, one for every main stakeholder.

Wow, isn't that way too much yearly training? I need to work! No, it's only seven modules. They may last half a working day; they could also be shorter, if they just involve updating the management on a known framework. Three-and-a-half days a year of training seems too much? Well, maybe this whole book is lost on you!

The real challenge is that leaders should not capture these principles, skills, behaviours and best practices just for their own sake. The Listening Leader will share what she has learnt with her staff, will enable them to benefit from her learning. This can be done by small town-halls, by an email including the main items that everybody needs to know, by encouraging exchange with the departments and databases able to provide more insights, by sharing their department's knowledge with the rest of the organisation.

There are companies who engage courageously on a journey reaching out to every single employee. BMW, the German car company, has trained more than 70,000 employees, among them many blue-collar workers, in what the main features of the company's brand, strategy and values are, in order to transform them into brand ambassadors.

dm, a German retail chain of drugstores, trains all of its new staff, including interns and apprentices, before they start the job they were hired for. In a process described as 'dialogical leadership',[11] the whole organisation constantly communicates in order to enable and finally empower all of its employees. A remarkable best practice: just walk into a dm store anywhere you find one, even if it's in a remote village on the east German countryside and you will find very authentic and helpful people, and not at all of the brainwashed kind. The dialogical leadership principles practised at dm are based on the individuals with their character, skillset, background and not on a standard model of customer-related behaviour.

Learn and teach to learn.

Can one learn and train empathy?

Research on leaders by Daniel Goleman and Richard Boyatzis demonstrated that sustainably successful managers required one-third skill and cognitive ability to two-thirds emotional intelligence. Yes, your eyes haven't betrayed you. More: sustainably successful *senior* leaders, have an increased ratio of 10 per cent level of intelligence to 90 per cent emotional intelligence.

So, don't look for excuses on empathy, such as, 'It's just a gene I don't have'. Ninety-eight per cent of people are able to empathise, our brains allow us to put ourselves into other people's shoes. But not all of us use this ability to its full potential.

In other words: empathy and emotional intelligence are ingredients of the successful Listening Leader and they can be learnt. And should be learnt.

What is empathy, actually? 'A person's endeavour […] to put himself in the situation of the other, and to bring home to himself every little circumstance of distress which can possibly occur to the sufferer […] in its minutest incidents.'[12]

And yes, we can train it. According to Roman Krznaric,[13] there are six habits of highly empathic people. If you want to enable yourself and your team to become more empathic, practise the following:

Habit 1: Switch on your empathic brain
Shifting our mental frameworks to recognise that empathy is at the core of human nature, and that it can be expanded throughout our lives.

Habit 2: Make the imaginative leap
Making a conscious effort to step into other people's shoes – including our 'enemies' – to acknowledge their humanity, individuality and perspectives.

Habit 3: Seek experiential adventures
Exploring lives and cultures that contrast with our own through direct immersion, empathic journeying and social cooperation.

Habit 4: Practise the craft of conversation
Fostering curiosity about strangers and radical listening, and taking off our emotional masks.

Habit 5: Travel in your armchair

Transporting ourselves into other people's minds with the help of art, literature, film and online social networks.

Habit 6: Inspire a revolution

Generating empathy on a mass scale to create social change, and extending our empathy skills to embrace the natural world.

If you put these six behaviours into your hand luggage you can start the journey to more empathy, a crucial ability for the Listening Leader.

Put the victim into the perpetrator's shoes

I used a rather simple tool to foster empathy. I called it *staff exchange*. In the terminology of the Center for Creative Leadership this would be 'challenging assignments'. That's the tool that brings about 70 per cent of our learning.

I described the principle as 'to put the victim into the perpetrator's shoes and vice versa', in order to go about it in a light-hearted, humorous way. Because we had neither real perpetrators nor real victims to deal with. Krznaric would call it Habit 2. The idea was to send people from my department to other areas we often interacted with, a subsidiary or another department in head office. It was not really understood by my HR colleagues at the beginning. They feared I would mean the typical expat programme, sending people abroad with an expensive package for two to three years. I hadn't finished speaking, when the 'but' was on the lips of my HR colleague. When she finished expanding on the high costs of these exercises and the budget constraints, I took a deep breath and explained that we were just thinking of a holiday substitution. When people would leave for a longer period (three or four weeks) they would be substituted for that time. The unit sending the replacement would still pay for her salary, the travel costs would be taken on by the unit sending the replacement, as well, while lodging would be taken over by the receiving unit. The first receiving unit's HR department was so slow to respond that we did everything like a family. The person replacing our US communicator when she was away stayed at her house in Washington and watered the colleague's garden in the family's absence. The point I want to make is: you can do staff exchanges for short periods and with low or no budget impact. What really matters is something different: the experience in the other person's position. The solicitor from the head office's legal department going to the subsidiary may find out that the letters he regularly sends from head office are perceived as stalinistic *ukas*, strict and abominable orders. He will moderate his language, in future, trust me. And his colleague from the subsidiary spending some weeks in head office will find out how big the pressure of regulators, the board and the public is on the chief counsel and why the central legal office needs to ensure strict following of procedures in subsidiaries. Hence the strict content of the letters. After this exercise head office will better explain why they have to demand certain procedures and will make sure the letters to the operating units are crafted in a transparent, pleasant and collegial tone.

Travel in your armchair

Emilio Salgari wrote wonderful books on the pirates in Borneo and I spent many hours devouring them. Enid Blyton's books followed suit. I was 12 and would read with a pocket lamp under my blanket. When, in 2011 I started planning my life after a high-energy corporate job that would finally end in 2015, one thing was clear from the beginning. My new life would have to allow me to reconnect to that pure joy I felt becoming a pirate or a boy involved in a secret investigation. I therefore organised my week in such a way that Mondays and Fridays are kept free from business meetings, coaching, advising and mentoring and are devoted to reading, reading, reading. And writing, too. I'm grateful to Roman Krznaric for providing me with a solid argument about increasing my empathy, when to me it's pure fun.

Should you like literature, art, film, online social networks as I love literature, give in to this liking, it will improve your leadership.

On visual stimulation: the big picture and scribing

As NLP teaches us, some of us prefer to use the language of feelings, others the visual, others again the auditive one. Remember this when it comes to enabling yourself and your team. It is surprising how many more people you can reach if you keep this in mind. A new craft was developed for business and political decision making in the last decade – graphic facilitation. It is about expressing even complex topics through illustration. Strategic workshops run according to the DesignShop, a format developed by the Americans Matt and Gail Taylor, applied by more and more organisations, among them Capgemini, Ernst & Young and the World Economic Forum in Davos. One of the scribes of Davos and ASE is Lucia Fabiani, whose illustrations you can find at the beginning of most of the chapters of this book. If you want to find out more about this technique and the philosophy of Big Picture illustration, look at the International Forum of Visual Practitioners' website, www.ifvp.org/.

Another good reason for diversity

'Diversity, diversity, diversity, I can't hear that word any more!' was the desperate explosion of a former colleague who put the issue into the wrong drawer, that of soft skills and political correctness trends. He was also an expert of mansplaining, that's when men interrupt women to tell that cute sugarbaby from the marketing department what *really* matters.

So, why on earth is there a diversity paragraph in the 'Enabling' chapter?

We have seen that 70 per cent of learning is actually experiential learning, or 'learning by doing'. Working in diverse teams (and it's not only about gender!) allows for many additional dimensions and perspectives on every single issue. Different perspectives allow enlightenment, transversal and lateral thinking; they enrich the conversation and therefore the ability to relate to very diverse stakeholders. If the job of the Listening Leader is to understand the stakeholders and bring their perspective into the company, they need to have many more antennae. That's what diversity can bring to the party.

Therefore, make sure your team is both diverse and cooperative. You need both a common understanding about the general tasks of your team in a cooperative attitude *and* very diverse team members.

When I first joined my employer's crisis committee we were eight members, all male, all Caucasian, seven of them middle-aged fathers of two, the eighth one a younger father with two children (it was me, then), seven out of eight were lawyers (I'm not). I immediately figured out, I was going to be the 'diverse' team member. Haha ... In many situations I discovered how much more effective our crisis committee became when we recruited women, when we had a much wider age spread, when the first psychologist joined, when non-Europeans joined the team. We got better by the minute. Different angles of a crisis could be identified, neglected stakeholders were brought into the picture, different cultural reactions to certain decisions were underlined. We simply became better.

Why is that so important for a successful communicative leadership? Because diversity as well as empathy are two very powerful tools to be excellent at interacting with all kinds of stakeholders. The more diverse the team the more stakeholders they can relate to. The more empathetic the team, the better they can put themselves into the stakeholders' shoes.

Learning in a diverse environment enriches the experience because there are more perspectives on one issue, because it can open your eyes on how some decisions may resonate with your stakeholders. Because you can't be man and woman, old and young, introvert and extrovert all at the same time.

For the Listening Leader it is essential to be able to hear the signals, weak or strong as they may be, to see red flags immediately, to verify the impact of his actions, to gather feedback, to prepare decisions, to test the waters. Remember, strategy is made of two parts: the vision of the leader and the company and the context, the environment. The excellent company is able to read the internal and external environment and to adapt to the changing scene to the benefit of its stakeholders.

Without a radar screen (empathy) you can't see the unidentified flying object. With Mr Spock, a half-alien in your team (diversity) you can identify the aircraft as coming from the planet Vulcan.

Why *diversity* really matters: it's not only about fairness and meritocracy, it is about the ability to be more empathetic with a multitude of stakeholders and therefore to act accordingly and succeed.

What a company can do to best enable its stakeholders

At the German electric giant Siemens there is an old saying: 'If only Siemens knew what Siemens knows.' The intelligence gathered in a company is never exploited to the maximum, that's an obvious truth. Important research has been devoted to managing the diffusion of knowledge in companies. Chief knowledge officers were established. I am not aware of a company who has solved this problem perfectly. I'm grateful for any hint.

Until I get this recipe for a Holy Grail feast, I'll suggest some crutches to start a company's journey with enabled staff towards communicative leadership.

1. Create a social platform within the company and let all of your employees access it.

2. Encourage knowledge sharing, through incentives, recognition.

3. Create a culture of openness, where every contribution is considered a valuable one.

4. Make knowledge sharing part of the leadership values and the objectives of the management.

5. Make sure knowledge-sharing enhancement (or lack thereof) in your team is measured in the yearly engagement survey.

6. Generate a collection of stories illustrating how the company works, what the educational and professional background of your people is, what they are working on and what successes and failures you have. Create transparency about the company's clockwork but do so with stories that illustrate why that certain wheel turns and in which direction it goes.

7. If you have the resources, bundle the knowledge and let your experts teach it to all the others – on finance, sales, marketing, operations, IT, product development, back and front office activities. And if you have more resources bundle this into a proper corporate university or academy.

On those academics so far away from practice...

Another sin I committed during most of my time in the hamster wheel was to consider research and academia as the bucolic home of intelligent people who had no clue how hard it is to earn a living with management. In the last four years in my 24/7 job I graduated from the Meyler Campbell Business Coach programme and carried out training for non-executive directors on mentoring. During those four years I was both continuing to manage global corporate communications at Allianz and learning. Both programmes were burdened with kilograms of reading. What looked like a duty to fulfil became a source of increasing joy and 'aha' moments. Many of the books I had to read and discuss with my peers in my tutorials are listed in the bibliography of this book. The readings, the discussions, my working papers, challenging the research with my practical working experience strongly improved my leadership. I became a better leader in the last four years of my corporate career and many of my direct reports and team members have told me so. Let's make a deal: I won't bother you with two or three paragraphs on this subject and you ponder this for a moment. If you can improve your performance as a leader *and* gain time and money by tapping into the brains and minds of academia, wouldn't you re-consider your opinion on what research can do to help you succeed? Try it, it's worth the experience. It may only be necessary to ask a gifted team member with a good academic background to prepare one or two sessions a year, where relevant research affecting your business, leadership, learning is shared with the whole team. And make some time for your own reading. It will pay off. Remember the 'discerning heart' that Solomon received. It also brought him richness and a long life.

Tools to discover preference and strengths

Preference

Myers-Briggs: The Myers-Briggs Type Indicator (MBTI) is the oldest preference questionnaire. Based on C.G. Jung's types it was developed in the 40s and 50s by mother and daughter, Isabel Briggs Myers and Katharine Cook Briggs.

The MBTI test allows you to find out which of the 16 basic personality types you belong to. This in turn allows you to relate to others, to effectively leverage your personality to reach your own way to higher performance.

The Listening Leader who has gathered some experience with the MBTI is well advised not only to know which personality type he or she is but also what staff members' personalities are and how to best use their different personalities for different tasks and different ways to fulfil them. For efficient enabling such knowledge can be game changing. The only downside is, not everyone can do this. You need to work with MBTI-trained coaches. In larger organisations you will normally find either MBTI-trained HR professionals or external consultants who can help.

To access the indicator, go to www.mbtionline.com/

For a good insight you may want to use both: Myers-Briggs to see which preferences you or your team members have and one of the following tests to see where your team's and your own strengths lie.

Strengths

StrengthsFinder: In 1998, the father of Strengths Psychology, Donald O. Clifton, PhD (1924–2003), along with Tom Rath and a team of scientists at Gallup, created the online StrengthsFinder assessment. It addresses 34 themes of personality from 'achiever' to 'woo', a person who loves to enthuse others. StrengthsFinder allows you to identify actions to leverage your strengths. You can buy the test online: www.gallupstrengthscenter.com/Purchase

Via: The Via character test has been developed under the direction of Martin Seligman, the father of positive psychology. Character types are derived from Seligman's research and range from A like Appreciation of Beauty to Z like Zest. It is free of charge and can also be taken online: www.viacharacter.org/www/The-Survey

LIFO: Based on the works of Erich Fromm, Carl Rogers and Abraham Maslow, LIFO focuses on necessary strengths for leaders, teams and individuals. It begins by identifying each person's basic orientation to life and work. Based on this information, it offers powerful learning strategies for greater personal productivity, increased influence with key people, and more effective teamwork. It is used to create self-awareness and provides opportunities for individuals to take steps to make personal changes. www.lifo.co/im-people-person/

Realise2: This online test also looks at your strengths and weaknesses and clusters them into four areas: realised strengths, unrealised strengths, weaknesses and learned behaviours. This last point is particularly interesting when you want to rebalance your energy, since these are areas you excel in because you learnt them with effort. But they cost you energy and don't always come naturally. Reducing the use of these skills allows you to also reduce the energy you spend on performing. To log in and purchase, go to: https://realise2.cappeu.com/4/login_public.asp

> ## Things to remember from Chapter 3, Enabling
>
> 1. Identify your strengths and those of your team.
> 2. Don't focus on weaknesses: foster strengths.
> 3. Focusing on strengths increases performance substantially.
> 4. Leverage motivation to increase performance.
> 5. Avoid 'groupthink'.
> 6. Train the big seven: strategy, customer focus, listening, crisis management, effective communication and presentations and integrated reporting.
> 7. Practice staff exchanges: low costs, high rewards.
> 8. Consider visual, emotional and auditive stimuli to better enable.
>
> And if you have mastered the art of enabling others you earned yourself the green belt. You are only two belts away from being a black-belt Listening Leader.

Enabling people: barriers to consider, according to a millennial

What are the limits and barriers to the achievement of enabling people?

1. **Identifying realistic development possibilities.** Let's start with the obvious. What if Charlie Chaplin's parents agreed with him that his best career would be one of basketball champion? As many hours he could have spent training, because of his height, he would never had reached this goal. And maybe the world would have lost an important comic actor. This shows you where the limits are, and those limits can be physical, but they can also be intellectual, psychological, characterial and so forth. When we speak about skills, both technical and 'soft', which are primary candidates for personal and professional development, things might not be as straightforward as you would imagine. Barriers might be intrapersonal conflicts of interest or seemingly unrelated but influential

factors. Along with my peers, I believe these hindrances can only feasibly be unearthed through dialogue. However, it would be silly to think everything will come up to the surface with a simple interested question. This is why leaders must approach such discussions with emotional intelligence, persistence and approaches tailored to the individual in question. To millennials, good leaders think of how to resolve these blockades themselves, but *great* leaders help their employees think them up. Only this way do you discover that the reason Rachel repeatedly shies away from giving presentations despite being an avid public speaker is a jokey comment a colleague made to her about her English, or that Paul did not progress as well in some of his international projects due to cultural differences he encountered when dealing with Chinese clients.

2. **Fear of losing investment in the employee.** I believe this to be one of the biggest dilemmas leaders and companies face today when it comes to enabling its workforce. On the one hand the war for talent is real. Being taken into consideration by these emerging talents as an employer requires a whole lot more than it used to only a few decades ago. A good old fishing rod does not suffice anymore to lure in those rare exotic fish. Instead, dangle in front of them promises of comfort, of work–life integration (often just a cover for merging the two, rather than healthy separation), of development. Once you've caught your highly educated parade fish, the real fight begins. Career patterns have changed enormously. Nowadays, who hasn't had at least three employers in the first career decade? Who doesn't know someone who has changed career *paths* before the age of 40? Companies feel the pressure to keep talent interested. That's why engagement and enablement have become buzzwords, which, when uttered, cause ears to prick up and heads to turn alertly from all corners of the room. On the other hand, I can hear the fist of a bitter manager hitting the table and his mouth pronouncing, 'It's all silly. They are sucking us dry of our resources and leaving us anyway. Why bother investing in them?' While it is easy to fall into the trap of panic regarding talent leaving regardless, I believe in many cases where this has happened, there was a lack of real communication between the leader and the talent. Excluding those rare manipulative individuals, for which probably nothing in

this book will ever work, people are willing to engage in honest conversations if they feel psychologically safe. If I knew I could talk to my boss about what things I would still like to do in my job in the next years, even if this meant considering leaving the company, the mere action of discussing it might open up options I had not considered. It seems to me that talking and thinking of strategies to deal with it are more likely to create opportunities, than avoiding such not strictly day-to-day-work–related topics.

3. **The daunting task of organisational restructuring.** Perhaps, when reading certain passages of this chapter, you might have found yourself thinking, 'Okay, well this is all well and good, but in order for these elements to be in place, you must have a very adaptable structure, something that my big company, with its silos and established practices does not have.' And yes, for sure, there are some solutions that are much easier to implement in a smaller, younger, flexible organisation. That might not necessarily be the case, though. One of the great opportunities companies ought to make use of in order to give employees the best possible tools to feel empowered is its network. Expertise, resources and experience often lie idle on the other side of the world or in a different department, while desperately needed in another. One easy way to create contact between the two, also called distributed intelligence, is through an enterprise social network (ESN). While many companies have an intranet or even an ESN, they often fail to fully harness its power. Maz Nadjm, a social media guru I was lucky enough to work with, opened my mind to the endless possibilities of the social network world within businesses. Ideas can range from logging all projects, with tags regarding skills, personal priorities and values, practical approaches to working according to preferences and personality types. The possibilities are endless. And you can either let your IT department set it up or, ideally, get the input of social media specialists who use knowledge about how humans think to structure a natural flow of information.

4. **Inappropriate means.** Even if you want to enable your employees and set up all the infrastructure to do so, it may not achieve your goals. We are moving from formal classroom and

e-learning training towards informal social and collaborative learning, where development and learning becomes intrinsically linked with job. Some of the new training trends that millennials feel at ease with are cooperative in nature:

- **Team-based learning:** In the hospital, medical apprentices walk together and are observed as each contributes bits of knowledge about the specific cases, therefore informing or reminding the others. Within companies, too, there is a huge knowledge base, which needs to be shared.

- **Experiential learning:** The experiences of employees within the company can be of huge benefit to others and can act as teachings. No other training is more tailored to your business reality than this.

  This method of training is great for millennials and non-millennials, as it leverages on the increasing range of different profiles employees have and partly or fully blends out technology, which can often be distracting. The active nature of these learning options engages employees, adding an additional layer of thinking, interpreting, voicing to the passivity of hearing, reading or watching.

5. **Gap between research and practice.** During my studies in the areas of organisational psychology, I learned a lot about what research is uncovering about optimal and suboptimal business practices. In my age-appropriately limited work experience, however, I found that despite these new insights derived from both laboratory and field studies in companies, therefore not, as some of you might think, removed from the real world, were not put into practice, especially in recruitment and selection processes. In many cases, managers in companies are not aware of these research findings and base their company practices on norms found in the industry.[14] An American study and a replication in the Netherlands about misconceptions about effective HR practices among HR managers and practitioners both found a significant discrepancy in knowledge.[15,16] The study quotes previous research finding evidence for the effectiveness of a link with academic advances for a company's financial and other well-being. While experience does account for something, it would be stupid to dismiss the valuable insights empirical research can provide. More widely speaking,

therefore, a company is advised to create a link with academia. This can start small, with leaders seeking subscriptions to leading scientific journals, or can go as far as organising monthly breakfasts with researchers and creating partnerships with universities and research institutes.

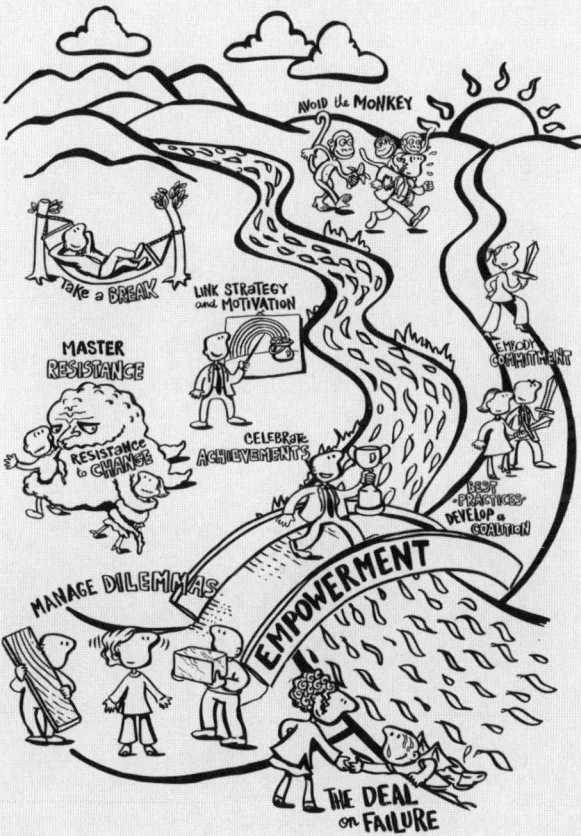

Empowerment: Deploy the energy of the stakeholders

- Why empowerment is not endangering good leaders but rather allowing them to grow through the process of sharing power
- What does 'power' mean to millennials and why the good old carrots and sticks have changed into the realisation of a calling and the fear of social isolation, today's drivers of reward and sanction or of motivation and fear.

Before we come to see how to best empower people, two premises are necessary. Good recruiting comes first. You need the right team in place, before you empower the wrong people. Or, as Dan Jacobs, Head of Talent at Apple, says in his remarkable French: 'I'd rather have a hole than an asshole.'

Second, the members of your team need to be engaged. Engagement stems from motivation, which, as we've seen, is made of autonomy, mastery and purpose. The level of engagement of your staff can be checked with an engagement survey, a rather common tool in most companies. If you have followed the journey of the Listening Leader so far, the odds that you have an engaged team are pretty good.

Underlying the relationship with your team is that rare commodity called trust. How to establish trust can be read in the Introduction.

The stage is set. Now let's see what empowerment is about.

What empowerment really means

Five to six hundred emails a day. Ten letters a day. Requests for information by journalists, calls for an exchange with peers of the company on a specific subject, meetings throughout the day from 8 to 8, twelve hours. That's a normal day for a busy manager. Very little to no time to take calls, no flexibility to manage the unexpected flying in on email. Not to mention continuous stimuli through social media. A tweet referencing you? You need to respond immediately. A discussion in a blog mentioning your function or yourself? Don't wait to respond! Everyone wants a decision from you. At least, so everyone thinks, including you: that's what you are paid for, as a manager. Always reachable, always ready to respond, always able to decide, on even the most complex conundrums being put in front of you. No wonder many managers feel exhausted when the week is over. And then there's their private life, where decisions also have to be pondered and taken.

That's how many good books gained formidable success. From the *One Minute Manager* by Ken Blanchard, years ago, to *Monkey Management* by Jan Roy Edlund or the one on the same subject by William Oncken as well as the bibles of efficiency by Stephen R. Covey. Excellent books on how to delegate, on how to avoid everyone pushing work on to your desk.

Whose fault is this hamster-wheel feeling? The organisation's business model? The lack of intelligence of the others? The reduction of staff at the cost of the survivors who now have to tackle much more work than previously, or what the company calls 'better productivity'? You can spend precious hours looking for those who caused this situation.

Take a breath and ask yourself: Do I have something to do with it?

It may well be.

As leaders, we want to be in charge. If we have to take responsibility for our function we need to know everything that happens in our departments. That's why we tell people we have to be copied in on emails. On how many of your 500 emails a day are you simply copied in? We want to manage the budget and the resources. That's why everyone asks us for permission to spend money and task people. How many of your daily decisions are about petty sums of the budget and the row between two of your teams on who is allowed to task Peter with that important project? How many of the daily meetings are really necessary to advance the company's objectives? And how many of those meetings did you call for?

Are you a bottle-neck for your team?

The problem with bottle-necks is that some organisations have a culture which supports this phenomenon, when 'the buck stops there'. Because the staff has given up on co-shaping its future and they have decided for themselves that the salary doesn't cover the risk of a failure. That every proposal is always rejected by the manager and therefore it doesn't make sense to put forward new ideas.

Organisations which tolerate this situation exist all over the world. There are basically two groups of them: the ones who will survive because they're protected, for example, because they are government agencies that have no competition, or monopolies that control a specific market; and private organisations, competing with other corporations. They will not survive. Their death may be slow and last a decade, but they are doomed to fail. They are slower, they are less motivated, they will breed burnt-out managers and scary employees, they won't be able to attract and keep good talents, to constantly reinvent themselves with new products and processes. Everything slowed down by the centripetal, absorbing machine of old power management.

The best answer of the old world was to delegate. Delegate comes from the past participle of the Latin verb *delegare* – 'to send as a representative'. You send a representative of your power to a meeting to *re-present* you, to replicate your power in that meeting.

That can be a very effective tool. Take your daily workload and split it up between your people by delegation. They can multiply your presence by replicating it in every situation. The limits of the powers of your staff members are those of the contract of delegation. They are there as a second Master's voice in a second place.

That works fine as long as the whole decision environment is stable. There is a clear position by everyone else, the business premise is clear and the choice may be simply digital, 'yes' or 'no'.

If you knew where your boss stood, you would simply have to voice his opinion. And for the boss it would be two decisions in the same moment, one by himself and the other by the person delegated to do so. The more staff you have and the clearer the context is, the easier it is to lighten your workload by delegating. That is, if it wasn't for such stupid facts such as the reduction of your resources and the lack of an infinite pool of people to delegate your power to. More so, that stability postulated for the system of delegation isn't there any longer. Facts, market conditions, stakeholders' expectations change so quickly that the delegated staff member needs to revert to the boss much more often: 'What should I say on your behalf?' You wouldn't accept a total reversal of your guidelines by a staff member, would you?

It's a question of power.

Remember, if this is all being tolerated and accepted in your organisation it means you are either working as a civil servant or you work in a company that will die some time, sooner rather than later. Leaving you without any power at all.

So you better manage the transition from delegation to empowerment.

Empowered people dare to take responsibility for their actions, not consulting the manual. Empowered people have discussed dilemmas with their peers and bosses and have an awareness about the strategy, which is the fine balance between different enthusiastic stakeholders to the benefit of both the company and the stakeholders. That's why they can decide. Remember the man who glued himself to the building of the insurance company (Chapter 3)? The empowered branch manager decided to deal with the situation with conventional wisdom and not desperately looking in the manual for the word 'glue'.

It's the sense of ownership held by the person to determine whether they are empowered.

On the benefits of empowerment

Why should I bother with empowering the team? It sounds risky. Should I really give away that little power I have earned with my sweat?

1. **It increases flexibility.** Your team can adapt swiftly to the changes in the stakeholder network. You gain speed by empowering your people, which is a major advantage in the VUCA world.

2. **It fosters innovation.** By allowing trial and error (see the 'deal on failures') it promotes different thinking, new ideas, innovation through connection with other functions and stakeholders.

3. **It unleashes the benefits of diversity.** Diversity is not a value per se, it serves the purpose of increasing empathy with the most different stakeholders. Empowerment allows those diverse talents to bring their peculiarities to bear in favour of a richer dialogue with stakeholders.

Empowerment boosters

Deploying the energy of the team can benefit from the turbo effect of some rather powerful tools, some of them very ancient, such as mentoring and some only recently refined to an art, like coaching (Figure 4.1). Let's look at how they can help us earn the brown belt of empowerment, the last hurdle before achieving the final black belt.

Business coaching

Oh, how I sinned, dear Lord! For years I thought I had been coaching the top management at Allianz. I advised them on good

Figure 4.1 The support for the Listening Leader

What is	
1. Coaching:	A relationship between a professional, properly educated business coach, a client (company employing the coachee) and a coachee or directly with a coachee. The coach pulls the best out of the coachee to improve his/her performance. The coach poses right questions, helps structure a problem and drives towards solution coming out of the coachee.
2. Mentoring:	A relationship between an experienced, knowledgeable employee (mentor) and an inexperienced or less-experienced employee (mentee). The mentee asks (pulls) and the mentor answers, advises, gives a second opinion, shares his/her experience with mentee. Initiative should come from the (active) mentee and the prompt reply should come from the (reactive) mentor.
3. Counselling:	An expert (i.e. communications, legal, strategy) advises a line manager without the specific functional knowledge of the expert.

communication. I gave them – hopefully precious – career tips. I motivated them to learn, be trained and try out new things. I warned them of stakeholders' complaints. I suggested updating the strategy to adapt to changes in the marketplace. And I called this 'coaching'. Poor me. One day a good old friend, Nancy Glynn, told me she had changed her career from a senior executive to a business coach. She wanted to become a coach and stop giving people advice but pull the best out of them. I felt a pain in my chest. Coaching is *not* about telling? No, it isn't, at least not non-directive coaching, the path she had chosen to pursue.

She was so energised by the Business Coach programme of Meyler Campbell in London that it was infectious and she has now become my supervisor. And when I was finally admitted to the same programme after an unforgettable conversation with Anne Scoular, the iconic founder of the Meyler Campbell institution and author of the *FT Guide on Business Coaching*, I started to discover I had been an imposter for many years. What I had done in the decades before my coaching education in London had been advising, not coaching. I was just an expert telling a general manager what options he or she had available. Coaching, instead, is about pulling the best out of the client in order to increase his or her performance. The client of a leader with a coaching approach is their employee.

As Anne Scoular writes about non-directive coaching: 'So mentoring, training, consulting, *put* in; coaching *pulls* out.'[1]

'Good business coaching is so powerful that if it was a drug, it would be illegal. A client walks into a coaching session stressed, overburdened, ready to give up – and an hour later emerges transformed: clear, focused, calmer, fit again to fight and win.'[2]

Coaching is not about coddling. Still some managers (fewer every new day, fortunately) believe that being coached means showing a weakness or that it is about feeling good. This is not the case. Good business coaching increases performance substantially. Coaching doesn't need to be bought solely from professional coaches. Leaders can become coaches too. The best schools (Harvard, Meyler Campbell and others) also offer programmes for line and staff managers who want to use coaching techniques to become better leaders.

A Listening Leader *is* a coaching leader.

Coaching can't be taught in a paragraph. But a short look at the most common model for a session of business coaching, or, if you want, for a conversation with your employee is GROW, developed by Sir John Whitmore. It illustrates the basic grid of a coaching conversation, shaped by a coach intensively listening for the largest share of this conversation, using her voice to ask stimulating open questions to answer the following four items:

Goal setting for the sessions as well as short and long term

Reality checking to explore the current situation

Options and alternative strategies or courses of action

What is to be done, **When**, by **Whom**, and the **Will** to do it.[3]

There are improved variations of the GROW model, like the Achieve Coaching Model.

What matters is that this process is carried out using the powers of good client questioning and intensive listening. A coaching cycle may last for a whole year. It's protected by confidentiality, it is contracted after a first chemistry meeting that allows client and coach to decide whether to enter into a coaching relationship. It is governed by ethical standards (see those of WABC, as an example, on www.wabccoaches.com). It should be non-directive (pulling, not pushing). It should be fully aware of the borders to psychotherapy. It is constantly improved by practise, peer exchange and supervision.

And it is awesome. The moment two people establish a *flow* that allows them to generate ideas, to gain new perspectives, to suddenly realise important insights leading to a solution to an apparently unsolvable problem on the job is a moment of bliss. That's what made me thank my employer for entrusting me with a leadership position. That's what makes me thankful for having undergone first-class training that allows me to coach top managers of multinational corporations facing enormously interesting challenges.

Supervision is key to good coaching. This involves having regular conversations with a peer and generally very experienced coach with whom to discuss difficult cases, figure out blind spots any coach can have, ethical questions and consult on a crucial issue that arises more often than not: 'Is this client in need of psychological consulting rather than just business coaching?'

Coaching strategy

Every company using business coaches for their employees should have a coaching way to have a greater impact. I'm not referring to the natural instinct of some HR officers to dictate a set of commandments on prices for business coaches, procurement guidelines and so on – all legitimate stuff but nothing to write home about. The use of business coaches within an organisation should be managed by individuals who understand the profession, the market and the added value that such an instrument can bring. If they don't, well, another lost opportunity for a badly run HR department.

I speak about the huge potential of insight that business coaches have and that remains untapped by companies, even by those who have professional HR practices and are used to working with coaches.

There are two things that a company can learn from the collectivity of coaches working with their staff:

- **Look behind – unveil the hidden state of the organisation.** Trends, red flags, hidden rules on the culture, the present stress levels and possible root causes, the implementation of new processes or the diversity policy. Without breaking their vow to confidentiality, coaches can share their insights on the company in an anonymised way, still providing the client company with relevant input of what is concerning their managers when they can vent their feelings in a safe environment.

- **Help to match personal motivation and purpose of the company.** It is important to constantly look for mutual benefits between the company and its management in terms of pursuing aligned purposes. The more the personal and corporate purposes are aligned, the higher the motivation will be and the more successful the company will get. Coaches are well trained to detect discrepancies and ask inspiring questions. You are well advised to consider another employment if you notice that the two purposes drift apart. Coaches aware of these shifts can be a very useful litmus test for both the company and the coachee.

Mentoring

Mentoring is when an experienced person guides a less-experienced person. Or, more formally: 'Mentoring is a formal or informal relationship established between an experienced, knowledgeable employee and an inexperienced or new employee. The purpose of the mentoring relationship is to help the new employee quickly absorb the organisation's cultural and social norms.'[4] Even beyond the world of employees, as mentioned in this definition of mentoring, mentoring can be applied across different organisation types, from advisory and supervisory boards, to start-ups and students.

When Popes die

When I was only 16 I was hired by a courageous woman, Franca Magnani. She was correspondent of the German TV ARD in Rome and she offered me the job of answering the switchboard in the afternoons, while doing my high-school homework. Two years later, on the 6th of August 1978, all hell broke loose when the most important thing that can happen in Rome occurred: the Pope, Paul VI had died. After 20 days a new Pope was elected, John Paul I. Portraits of the new pope were produced for the TV station and after some weeks of intense work the exhausted journalists and cameramen took some days off to recover the August holidays that, because of the events, had been cancelled. So, when on the 28th of September suddenly the new pope died, there was nobody in the offices of the German TV to go on air to give the news to the German public. Except for me and a cameraman, Abo Schmid. I was a rookie, had just turned 18 and had never stood in front of a camera. But I was the only one there in those first hours. So I had the honour of breaking the news myself. In the next few hours Franca and the others would be back and I would return to my humble duties. But when everything was over and I left to go back to school and finish my stint at the TV I asked Franca how I could ever thank her appropriately for this wonderful opportunity and trust that she had given me. And she answered: 'Don't thank me. Should you make a career, help younger people as I helped you.'

With Franca I had found the first of my many mentors whose wisdom and guidance I have enjoyed over the years. A good mentor can be life changing. Become one yourself. A Listening Leader is also always a mentor.

A mentor is more senior and is there to answer questions by the mentee. A good mentoring relationship is based on the initiative being taken by the mentee to engage the mentor in questions where the experience, skillset and knowledge of the mentor is used to improve the performance of the mentee. Needless to say that mentors benefit enormously from good mentees: they're being asked the relevant questions they may not reflect enough about. They may be confronted with fresh, different views. They may benefit from a totally diverse perception of the business reality and thereby gain new insights.

Cross-mentoring

A very effective way to increase the performance of your staff is to engage in cross-mentoring. This is when someone from one unit or department mentors someone from somewhere else, also across different companies (unless they compete). This has the advantage of further enlarging the horizons, to see how things can be done differently in different environments.

Diversity mentoring

Sometimes mentoring programmes are based on the diversity between mentor and mentee (except for the seniority, also diversity in terms of gender, ethnic background, educational background, age etc.). This is still an additional dimension of the enlargement of horizons and the expansion of experience well beyond one's normal cultural and social borders – for both mentor and mentee.

Functional mentoring

A lawyer reasons differently from a mathematician or a violinist. Or maybe not? Try it out by mentoring across functions. Especially when specific areas of an organisation need to work more closely in spite of a very different set of tasks, cross-functional mentoring proves very useful. The sales department may have a compliance issue: sometimes insurance company sales agents do misselling and this is heavily sanctioned by the company and by law enforcement. Having mentors from the compliance department mentoring salespeople and the other way around can be an effective way of increasing the understanding between these two areas and one of the many tools used to change behaviours.

Reverse-mentoring

Reverse-mentoring occurs when a more junior person mentors a more senior person. It could be on digital matters, for example. Read the reverse-mentoring my millennial daughter Clementina gives the baby-boomer father advocating communicative leadership at the end of Chapter 5.

Your role as a Listening Leader is to establish whether someone in your team would benefit from mentoring and, if so, from which kind of mentoring.

As per all the other disciplines that the Listening Leader needs to master (information, communication, enabling and change), empowerment also has its tools. The most powerful ones I just described, coaching and mentoring.

Six empowerment tools

Coaching and mentoring are the two crown disciplines of empowerment.

I have six more tips to speed up the empowerment of your staff:

1. Strike a 'deal on failures'.
2. Redistribute power.
3. Link strategy to intrinsic motivation.
4. Learn to deal with dilemmas.
5. Have a break: let others lead.
6. Avoid the monkey.

The 'deal on failures'

'We either learn to fail or we fail to learn', says Harvard psychology professor and author, Tal Ben-Shahar.

One of the biggest obstacles to people taking on responsibility and acting as empowered corporate representatives is the fear of failing.

Attitude and culture are tantamount for a 'learn from failure' environment. And you have to lead by example: *Be a healthy optimist* and not a negative perfectionist.

If you have a *clear set of rules*, of dos and don'ts, you can always revert to the rulebook to take decisions and let the responsibility remain with the power that delegated you to represent it.

Is this enough? No, because this will not allow you to enthuse your stakeholders.

Strike a deal with your staff – but *don't forget the other stakeholders*: What happens when we fail with customers? Do we become defensive? Do we regularly assess the impact of this failure on stakeholders? How do we reduce or eliminate the impact of this failure? Do we apologise? Do we share our learnings with the stakeholders?

Is this enough? No, because this will not allow you to enthuse your stakeholders.

Make sure you *discuss failure within your team*. Dedicate a team meeting to the contract you want to sign with your team, the 'deal on failures'. How shall we deal with the responsibilities for failure and how do we learn from failures? Address all open issues and create a simple set of rules, ideally not more than five or six, something like:

1. We learn from failures.

2. We volunteer any information concerning a failure; we address mistakes proactively.

3. We don't judge; we try to listen attentively and strive to understand.

4. The standard is set by the manager who leads by example.

5. We accept the emotions that go with the failure instead of immediately trying to 'fix it'.

6. We assess the impact of the failure on every stakeholder.

Every failure dealt with according to these jointly developed rules will not be sanctioned but rewarded. A bonus? A recognition? The task to lead the next project? Your call, depending on the motivational structure of your team.

What matters is not necessarily the wording of your 'deal', it's the attitude and spirit of the team and their participation in crafting those rules, in their *ownership* of the deal.

Harry's choice: Sometimes the rulebook doesn't allow for the necessary flexibility to meet customers' demands. Let's see what empowerment meant to me and my family during a recent trip to Australia.

The One&Only Hayman Island in Australia is one of the most beautiful resorts on this planet. When I arrived there with my wife and three-year-old we were astonished by the fact that the 'family room' we had booked consisted of two huge separate rooms, when we really only needed one. The term 'family room' suggested one single space, while here there were two large ones. We immediately said we would not need the second room and gave back the key to the second room. Everything had been paid in advance and my travel agent told me to forget about receiving a refund, that their terms and conditions were very clear. Everything else was wonderful in this resort, the room, the service, the food, the weather, the unbelievable beauty of the landscape and the sea life and we truly enjoyed our time there. But that one stubborn and counterintuitive reaction by the resort prompted me to ask to talk to Harry, one of the hotel managers. It was immediately clear that legally I was not entitled to a refund. But it was also very clear to him that I was disappointed by the scratch on the otherwise perfect surface of the resort. Harry made it happen and he promised I would get a refund. When I told my agent what had happened, she said: 'His boss will crucify him, they never give refunds.' A couple of days later I met Harry's boss and he simply said: 'If Harry thought it was right to give you the refund, he must have had a good reason to break the rules. Please continue to enjoy the stay with us.' This turns a happy customer into an enthusiastic customer.

Harry is lucky to work in a company and with a boss who allows him to expand his own perimeter of power and responsibility to fulfil a promise of bliss for the customer.

But what if the boss had indeed crucified Harry as my travel agent had suspected? If Harry had made a mistake?

The way we deal with mistakes and failures, even the smallest ones, may be a key criterion to kill or grow the proper culture that nourishes communicative leadership. Mistakes occur all the time – the real challenge is to make sure that you are aware of the mistake, that you truly understand it, before you start thinking of how to fix it. Learn what happened in order to learn how *not* to do things.

Counselling

When you advise someone who is not an expert in your field, you are counselling this person. That's what communications people normally do with CEOs or lawyers.

Anne really blew it. She put the list with all the salaries of her department, including the compensation of her boss, into the fax machine and pushed the short-dial function for their tax accountant. Or so she thought. A second look at the short-dial list and her heart dropped to the floor of the copy room. She didn't send the salaries to the company's accountant, she had just revealed the compensation of the whole team to a business partner.

She saw no alternative but to go to her boss, spill the beans and quit, which is what she did. Her boss responded by telling her: 'Anne, as of next week I'm going to raise your salary by 10 per cent.'

She couldn't believe her ears. Her manager simply said: 'You immediately came clean. You are brave. You take responsibility for what you do. You know how to deal with failures. This has to be rewarded.'

Anne had just witnessed a Listening Leader in action.

Years later, after a traumatic insolvency of her own firm, Anne Koark, a brave English entrepreneur now living in Munich, recovered from her business failure in such a remarkable way that her book on insolvency and what she learnt from it, climbed the bestseller list and stayed there for a long time.[5]

If you play the blame game, not only are you not a Listening Leader, but, much worse, you are risking your job. Next time people may try to hide the mistake, blame someone else or simply avoid making decisions. This will backfire on you. And turn a mistake into a failure, a small lie becoming a big lie.

How one can effectively learn from failure is the sense of another interesting story my coaching friend Claudia Danser recounts:

Before joining the BBC, Wayne was a young producer at Granada. ITV asked him to refresh one of their biggest long-running shows, *The Krypton Factor*. They wanted it to be more like one of their newest shows that was a success with a younger audience. Wayne and the team set about making changes to several elements including a crazy assault course and produced a show quite removed from the original. In the edit, Wayne knew they'd gone too far. He was right. The day after the first show aired, he received a call in the early morning from an elderly lady who told him he had ruined their family's favourite programme. It was the first of many. The viewer complaints flooded in and the show was never commissioned. After airing for 17 years, Wayne and the team's revamp had killed *The Krypton Factor*. Now Wayne could have wallowed in this and thought his career to be over. Instead, he embraced the mistake and learnt from it. He subsequently worked for the BBC and was asked to update the popular but declining *Question of Sport*. Everything he got wrong on *The Krypton Factor* enabled him to do things right at the BBC. His almost career-ending failure gave him the insight of how this time around he needed to do things differently to succeed. First, Wayne and the team sat down to think about the show's core values. Only then did they make changes, changes that fitted those values. The changes were slight and cosmetic to update the show rather than totally reinvent the format. In this way, they retained the programme's loyal audience and built on it. Eighteen years later, a *Question of Sport* remains a success and continues to air as one of the BBC's most well-loved shows. When Wayne became Head of Entertainment at the BBC, he continued to use this approach to failure with a new team working on shows for Saturday nights. They developed and produced several ideas together that didn't work. Learning from this, Wayne and his team along with the BBC's commissioning team created and produced *Strictly Come Dancing*. It became a huge award-winning hit, a No. 1 show running for more than 13 series not only in the United Kingdom, but also in the United States and over 40 countries worldwide, where the show is also locally produced. Without previous failures, *Strictly Come Dancing* could never have come about. And this is why Wayne

▶

believes that as a creative manager, it's important to empower your team to fail and not to micro-manage them. As a creative leader, you know that some of your team's ideas will work and some won't. But you have to let your team create and see for themselves how and why it fails. They need to have their own 'a-ha!' moment in order to truly benefit from the learning. If you tell them, they won't mess it up and won't learn. They will also stop listening to you. Failure is the most important part of everyone's growth and education and is a crucial part of being a successful, creative Listening Leader like Wayne.

Redistribution of power

How to divide up power and turn it over to the bottom of the organisation may be considered an art, but basically it's a skill you can learn.

- First comes a brief reflection on what powers you have in your role.
- Then comes the litmus test of character: How much of this is really your prerogative and how much can you cede to your staff in order to allow them more freedom?
- Third, try out if it's working and if not, adapt it.
- The most important thing to do, however, is to ask your team: What do you need from me to be more effective and take decisions that advance our objectives and save us time?

Now, and only now, you can start thinking about how you ensure that things don't get out of hand and you are kept abreast of developments that you finally have to sign for with your own boss.

Link strategy to intrinsic motivation

To deploy the full power of enabled team members there is a seamlessly endless source of energy: the motivation of your people. The motivation is at its best if it is in keeping with the purpose of the company. This is why recruiting the right people is so important. To recruit, develop, enable and empower the right people you have to get to know them and check whether they match the company. Both partners need to be aware of the purpose of the other. The popular business writer John Strelecky calls it the 'Purpose for Existing' that needs to be aligned between staff member and company.[6]

Learn to deal with dilemmas

In trying to avoid mistakes one looks for a grid allowing us to know what the right thing is: it's either good or bad and you should follow the good path. What a nice world IT managers have created for themselves. The core of the billions of actions that their systems spark off is based on the simple alternative 1 or 0, yes or no.

But the world isn't that simple. Balancing different stakeholders is a daily exercise where no rule-book can tell you what is right and what is wrong.

I sometimes ask my students to enter into a dialogue with me on some questions of general interest. Then I ask them to tell me whether they are in favour or against child labour. No hand is raised to defend child labour, of course. Then I ask them whether they have ever seen a picture of a child on the lap of a sturdy Western tourist in a Thai brothel in some news magazine. Or maybe the picture of a child-warrior from the Ivory Coast. Or whether they have heard of young boys in Laos, Cambodia, Myanmar or Vietnam selling opium and becoming addicted themselves in order to become reliable salespeople for the organised crime. These are all child labourers. The families of these children need money. Now, is there a difference between being forced to kill, prostitute or become a drug addict for money and sewing leather footballs in terms of psychological and physical impact on these children? When my students nod, I ask them if they could approve of child labour that has no impact on their health and that would only last four hours a day plus four compulsory hours of schooling every day. When the first student understands and suddenly defends the soft version of child labour, I stop the enthusiasm reminding them I didn't want to make them change their mind in favour of some sort of child labour. What matters is the reflection on the matter. Considering the causes of child labour, the poverty, the fight for survival of families and the different intensities of exploitation of a child. This conversation is what matters.

Every day in companies dilemmas arise between stakeholders, between the interests of the shareholder and of the customers, between the interest of the employee and that of the consumer and so on. There very rarely is a digital answer, 'yes' or 'no'.

How to deal with dilemmas

The best way to deal with the dilemmas is to make them explicit to both parties, to all involved stakeholders. Why is there a difficulty of choice? Which commitments (to the customer, to the capital markets etc.) can turn into conflict?

All affected parties should be:

- aware of the positions of all involved parties including their goals and objectives
- open to accepting the realities and constraints, analysing the context and the relevant players
- ready to discuss options and choices with their consequences.

They can mutually decide whether to tolerate, to accept the counterpart's position or whether to change their own position, strike a deal, a trade-off or simply walk away as customers or employees. It is necessary, though, to understand where the other person comes from, what objectives they have, what values, time constraints and so forth. In other words, you may have guessed, to listen to their concern. Even if you can't reach an agreement, at least you can learn to accept the other's point of view. A brilliant book has been written by the Ghanaian-American philosopher Kwame Appiah about dealing with the modern, global dilemmas we're increasingly faced with.[7]

Have a break: let others lead

I've been there: a control-freak gifted with constructive paranoia, always on the prowl to listen to weak signals and prepare my company to deal with them. The smartphone always turned on, 24/7/365, night and day, on the job and on vacation. There's a nice German song from Tim Bendzko, called 'I just have to quickly save the world.' It goes like that:

I would have loved to be there, but I'm so busy. Let's talk later. They need me out there, the situation is underestimated. Maybe our lives depend on it. I know you mean it and you can't do without me, but don't worry, I'm not going to be away for long.

I just have to save the world, then I fly to you. I have to check 148,713 emails, who knows what's going to happen, because so many things are going on. Let me just quickly save the world and then I'll be with you.

I admit, I sometimes felt like the guy from this song or Atlas, with the burden of the whole world resting on my shoulders. The brave boy I've always been, I would always be on duty. I am irreplaceable, of course.

For a number of reasons I decided to quit Allianz in 2011 and had agreed with the CEO that I would leave six months after his successor would have taken office. The date of the change at the helm wasn't clear, but his current contract would expire at the end of 2014 and I had some time to deal with a couple of challenges and prepare my exit. One of the tasks to address was to find some good candidates for my succession. Incidentally, the company was on a journey to improving work–life integration and intended to promote sabbaticals. But no one in the top management had ever taken a sabbatical.

I was tired and strained by almost two decades of permanent duty, I needed to find a successor, no top manager was available to take a sabbatical and state an example: a wonderful coincidence. So I asked for a sabbatical, which was granted. And I decided to take a month off every year in summer for the rest of my time in the company. Good opportunities to test candidates for my succession. Turning off my smartphone and seeing whether I really was irreplaceable.

I wasn't, of course. The colleagues taking over in my sabbatical and the longer holidays could try out my job. And my boss and his executive board colleagues could test them, see them in action. Without a puppeteer in the backstage, since I started to enjoy holidays without daily interruption and crisis calls. You all know what happened: the world did not collapse, the planet didn't need me to be saved. I could identify a couple of candidates for my succession, they were tested by the C-suite and when I left, a brilliant successor was chosen and I am long forgotten. With the additional reward of four marvellous summers.

Let go from time to time. It pays off.

How to get and give the break

Are you one of those stressed managers I described at the beginning of this chapter? Have you ever had the impossible dream of taking a sabbatical? Or of doing an MBA? Or of increasing your already stellar performance with good business coaching? Have you been asked by your partner to take a parental leave? If you have answered 'yes, but I don't have the time' to these questions, you may have good reason to read these lines.

Of course you have the time. Not only that, but if you do take this time to learn or recharge your batteries or spend a particularly important period caring for your sick parents or helping your partner to manage private challenges, not only will you do something that matters greatly to you or that positively impacts your health, but you also get to empower your own people. A *sabbatical* is a wonderful opportunity to test someone from your team: can you take over while I'm on a sabbatical? What unique training for that person; what a growth opportunity, a learning occasion. Kill two birds with one stone: enjoy a break and develop your people. *Maternity* or *paternity* leaves are another great opportunity to gain time for your family and let someone else in your team take over and learn. Let others lead while you're off on your summer *vacation*.

If you do so, discuss a questionnaire with the person substituting you – questions for an anonymous survey after that period in order to gather feedback about this leadership experience. Or simply both take a 360-degree survey.

Avoid the monkey

Imagine you're rushing to a meeting you don't want to be late for. Suddenly Susan is in your way. Yesterday you had given her a task she has to deliver by next week – nothing spectacular, a small report. She stops you to complain about the complexity of the task and how much she has on her desk and – look! – how the first numbers she calculated don't add up . . . you sigh and think how easy that task is. In half an hour you would manage to do what Susan fears not being able to do in a week. You tell her you will prepare the report yourself. Susan has just given you the monkey, uploading further burden onto your shoulders.

The exact opposite of empowerment is having new monkeys to manage every day. People will off-load their tasks onto you if they're not empowered. Empowerment allows them to shape their day, their agenda and to take stock of their new freedom to better serve the company, take better decisions, listen and respond more efficiently. Empowerment therefore allows you to avoid the monkeys, work less, grow and develop your staff members. While accepting the monkey will lead straight to overwork, burn-out, stress and dissatisfaction for you, the leader.[8]

A good company empowers its leaders

Empowerment, unlike information or communication, cannot be practised in an isolated way in a company. Of course, information and communication are impoverished and the impact on the company's profit minimised if they are practised by individual leaders only. Empowerment only deploys a significant impact if the whole company practises it.

To have a real impact, empowerment has to be specifically addressed in the leadership guidelines or values of the company. The company has to state clearly that 'Leaders of this company actively empower their staff to take on responsibility, act on behalf of the company and listen to stakeholders channelling back these inputs to the top management in order to change the company for the better', or something along these lines. Empowerment has to be empowered.

Once this intention is stated you can ask your employees in the yearly engagement survey: 'Has your manager actively empowered you this year?' 'Has the company actively empowered its staff this year?' and a couple of other related questions and you get a picture of where the company stands on implementing empowerment. You can regularly monitor the empowerment, measure it.

Good empowerment can be incentivised, but need not be . . .

Once you measure the efforts to foster empowerment through the engagement survey, you can easily incentivise empowerment of management by linking parts of the variable compensation to the results of the engagement survey. There is a cheaper way, though. When the Chairman empowers the CEO and the CEO empowers his direct reports, the avalanche of success has started. The empowerment process is so stimulating and motivating for the empowered person that it may not need to be incentivised with material means. It's like getting rid of an unwieldy weight on your shoulders. Suddenly walking is almost like floating. This feeling will be more exciting than a material incentive.

Adieu à la résistance

We all know resistance to change. When we have to do something that is different than usual, a psychological barrier is likely to arise. Habits, routines and repeated behaviours are a safe ground on which to walk, since they do not draw on extra resources from our mind. Therefore, a sort of defence mechanism is activated when a change occurs. Every team or organisation going through change has to acknowledge that change is always accompanied by resistance.

Dealing with change resistance is a slightly more complicated issue than acknowledging its existence. Resistance comes in many different disguises, from passive inertia to active sabotage. Secondly, it can evolve over time, become more or less pronounced in different areas of the organisation. Thirdly, resistance is closely linked to loss of trust and credibility. Gaining them back is much more difficult then losing them.

To deal effectively with change resistance, an organisation needs to sit down and analyse. Its leaders need to be aware of the form of resistance related to the specific change they are introducing. Running a listening analysis helps to reveal the pockets of opposition and to create a first mapping in order to address them. Sometimes, resistance is typical and linked to emotional states (e.g. fear of something new, fear of leaving the comfort zone, fear of ideas being questioned). Some other times it is rooted in factual causes (e.g. this change will bring more work). Other times again, it depends on organisational particularities (e.g. past changes, opportunities and threats perceived, etc.). Further, resistance to change is directly influenced by the leader's actions: a Listening Leader needs to *understand* the resistance in order to address it. Here are the five things a Listening Leader needs to do to tackle change resistance:

1. **Constantly communicate with people**, listening to their needs in order to further engage them.

2. **Personally embody the real commitment** of the organisation and **be a role model** in order to lead by walk-the-talk.

3. **Develop a leadership coalition with peers** in order to create an effective alignment among the leaders of the organisation.

4. **Be open and look at internal and external best-practices** in order to benefit from other experiences and accelerate the change.

5. **Celebrate positive achievements** to support people in order to generate enthusiasm around the possibility to succeed.

The primacy of common sense

Empowered employees can be the nightmare of every control freak in an organisation, and especially for every control freak in the C-suite or the corporate communications department. The leeway that empowerment leaves to unorthodox behaviour may possibly threaten the reputation of the company. But not if it is guided by common sense. Common sense is the currency of all stakeholders, the benchmark against which the court of public opinion decides. This is the real safety belt for control freaks: you can stand any public heat if what you did as a company corresponds to common sense.

A good way for you to have the right compass for common sense is by surrounding yourself with people who have a good sense of what conventional wisdom is. Ideally that's your partner or best friend or a trusted family member. Ideally it's someone who has a totally different job and may not understand the intricacies of your business.

I call it 'the spouse's test': what would your partner, who has no clue about your business environment, say about this decision?

And now it's almost time to put the rubber on the road of communicative leadership. But first comes the millennial's view on power. Now, with the brown belt of empowerment you are one belt away from the black belt of the Listening Leader. Yes, I know, I'm missing the blue belt, but I'm sure the well-hearted judoka among the readers will forgive me.

Things to remember from Chapter 4, Empowerment

1. Strike a 'deal on failures'.

2. Understand motivation and link it to strategy.

3. Learn and teach how to deal with dilemmas.

4. Have a break: let others lead.

5. Avoid the monkey.

6. Master resistance.

7. Mentoring is a more senior person advising a more junior person. Or the other way around. Both benefit from mentoring.

8. Be a coaching leader and use coaching to increase performance.

A millennial's view on power

Millennials, as an already significant part of the workforce, are strong supporters of empowerment and what it means for workplace dynamics as well as creativity. They feel confident in their own approach and would like to be given the opportunity to work according to individual needs, as they believe this produces the best work. They are energised by the prospect of taking on new responsibilities and they try to impress accordingly.

In order to understand fully what this mindset entails, let's take a closer look at the dimensions of power that millennials are grappling with.

Structure

Autonomy and flexibility are hailed as the non plus ultra for millennials. And this is true. But only if there is underlying structure. With that I don't mean bureaucratic processes, or a step-by-step guide to each task. We are instead talking about the framework. Employees of this generation like to work knowing the values of the company, its goals and specific project aims, the expectations from stakeholders towards them and deadline details. Whether they are working towards a specific professional plan or not, they like to know their options, so career progression prospects are of interest to millennials.

However, what they would like to put their personal footprint on, mostly regards the approach to work. This can include dress code, structuring of working day or week, modes of learning and working. We are possibly a little egocentric, it's true, but it also means we have evaluated our own preferences and talents and entered the workforce with a good idea of how we work best. We would probably not so easily accept a company culture of 'This is the way we do things around here.' We would ask: 'Can I do it my way if I still deliver?'

Identity

Labels. We hate them. Many millennials might not even want to be called millennials. One day we might be actively opposing factory farms, the next our fighting spirit is targeted towards cyber-spying. But we might neither be vegetarians, nor hippies.

Rather than belonging to specific groups, we identify with principles or strategies of many of them, and accept the fluidity of our identity. This enables us to see problems from different angles and to apply knowledge from different perspectives to issues at hand. The coupling of entrepreneurial and business sense with societal issues is just one example.

Collective intelligence

Global digital connectivity has allowed us to gain great conscience about world issues. Armed with not just ideals or abstract concepts, but also a sense of reality and a strong backing from the community, we feel entitled to challenge the big powerhouses. It is interesting to see how our mistrust towards these holders of power and the scepticism meet the idealism of youth and optimism, which is born out of the possibilities available to us today.

We can start our own companies and provoke action through the airing and discussing of our opinions on social media. We can also plan for alternatives to the concentration of power we see today. There is this belief in collective power among us, which has surely been shaped by our connectedness online. It is also the power we see as most legitimate. While previous generations might have accepted that seniority, age or experience in part legitimate power, we strive for meritocracy and democracy.

In our opinion, the best work is achieved by building upon each other, utilising each other's strengths and evaluating issues from different points of view, be they cultural, educational or personal. The global exchange between people has also allowed us to increase our knowledge about cultural differences and be tolerant and understanding towards these differences. This might impact different ways to go about empowering your stakeholders in a very collectivistic or in a pronounced individualistic environment, in more egalitarian rather than more hierarchical societies and cultures.[9]

Power goes hand in hand with responsibility

Tainted by scandals and horrid shows of abuse of power, there is now increased focus on the responsibilities that come along with power. As mentioned above, this generation is acutely aware of the issues that affect today's and tomorrow's world, be they social or environmental or about human and civil rights. It is unbelievable to us (perhaps this shows our naivety) that the big deciders in the world fail to tackle these issues. Just think that only 42 per cent of young Americans support capitalism today.[10] If this mindset is maintained and channelled correctly, this could mean a revolution in power structures and exertion: The question of who decides what and how, in the world of tomorrow.

Chapter 5

COMMUNICATIVE LEADERSHIP
THE JOURNEY of the LISTENING LEADER
The CEO MATTERS!
COMMUNICATION
REPORTING ON and TO ALL STAKEHOLDERS
LISTEN!
BE HOLISTIC
INTEGRATED REPORTING
ENABLING
AVOID the MONKEY
WIN THE AUDIENCE
BE RELEVANT
READING the SPEAKER
WARM & COLD COMMUNICATION
THINK the BIG SEVEN
LINK STRATEGY and MOTIVATION
BE FAST
ALL FACTS on the TABLE!
PLAIN LANGUAGE!
FACTS
INFORMATION
DON'T MANIPULATE
BE SPECIFIC
ENTHUSE CUSTOMERS
TAKE a BREAK
MASTER RESISTANCE
RESISTANCE to CHANGE
MANAGE DILEMMAS
EMPOWERMENT
THE DEAL on FAILURE

The Listening Leader in action

- How to go about changing your leadership, practically.
- How to make use of change management techniques to advance your cause.
- How practising *communicative leadership* will allow you to combine success with personal satisfaction and earn the black belt of the Listening Leader.

You are reaching the final miles of this marathon. Now you have to ask yourself whether you want to let this book serve its purpose and do something about your leadership or whether you want to go back to business as usual.

I've tried to explain why communicative leadership makes business sense. Why it especially does so in today's volatile economic environment and in the presence of media-empowered citizens, customers, investors and employees.

Chapters 2 to 4 described the journey to becoming credible with your stakeholders, the establishment of a dialogue with them, the necessary efforts to discover the energies of the stakeholders and pull the best out of them and finally the deployment of the troops, empowered and responsible, ready to manage change.

The seven steps to becoming a Listening Leader

Every marathon starts with a first step. There are seven steps to be walked to enact communicative leadership. The first is about your awareness.

Step 1: Look for your triggering event

At some point you have to start to engage on the journey to becoming a Listening Leader, should you share the basic ideas of communicative leadership. When is the best moment? I could simply say: now. But that's too simple and would not work. Think hard and try to identify the moment when you decided to change your leadership style. Or create it now.

Observe the world around you: where have you seen extraordinary customer service? Where have you seen lousy products? When were you last upset about a company and why? Make this the starting point of your own change. It will allow you to revert to this initial question, this triggering event, when things start to seem complicated. Remind yourself of what was the starting point of your change.

A wise old man kicks me off

Another visit from a consultant. I always dreaded people coming to sell my company consulting services. I loved to work under budget constraints because it sharpens the skills of those within the company. So, I had very little external budget and I very often blessed my self-constraint, since it allowed me to finally say 'no' to a proposal, 'it's just not in the budget'. But this person was different. Heinz Goldmann was his name and I owe him so very much. He left Germany as a boy before World War II because he was convinced that it was not a safe place for Jews. His father, who fought for Germany in World War I, could not understand the apprehension of young Heinz. Unfortunately, the boy, who later served in the American Army and freed Germany from the Nazis, was right. His parents were murdered in a concentration camp. Heinz came back to Germany after the war and he imported the latest trends in marketing and communication. He was terribly expensive (tongue-in-cheek he once said: 'That's my little revenge on the Germans') and I finally hired him to carry out training for our whole executive board. He was stellar. He taught me the importance of EMMA, an acronym I first heard from him. He taught me the importance of good listening. That day, it was in the late 1990s and I was in the middle of a very demanding job challenge. I went to the entrance of our main building in Munich and picked him up. In the short walk to my office, this small but very fit old man (he was already 80) just walked next to me, without speaking a word. I made some small talk and hastened to my office. Then he stopped. I had to stop, too, and I turned to him with a question in my eyes. He said: 'Emilio, you are under severe stress. You are like a candle burning from both sides. If you want to reach my age and my fitness, you better think about slowing down.' It came out of the blue and I looked baffled. 'How do you know?' I stuttered. He said: 'It's the way you walk. I just happened not to listen to what you were saying and was just focused on your steps, your back, your shoulders. I saw a big burden.' This man had listened, but not to my words; he had listened to my body. I asked him whether one could learn this. 'Of course one can.' That was my triggering event to reinvent myself as a manager, striving to become a leader, without knowing, yet, what a Listening Leader would be.

Step 2: Increase your self-awareness and assess yourself

The first thing you need to do is to become aware of where you stand. Analyse your strengths, your motivation, your talents, your calling. At the end of Chapter 3 you'll find the most common strength analyses and tests.

To start this journey take the test you feel most comfortable with. Ideally you have someone to discuss this with and get an outside opinion on the results. Get new perspectives on you. If you have a 360-degrees tool in your company, go for it. Try to find out as much as you can about yourself. It sounds like a paradox, but you can learn surprising things about yourself.

Remember the recommendations for self-enabling listed at the beginning of Chapter 3:

- Be aware of yourself and your context.
- Know your strengths and weaknesses.
- Be mindful.
- Be focused and practise equanimity.

Become aware of yourself, of your style, of the impact you have on people, of your strengths.

This book is about communicative leadership. The term itself may scare people off. As we know there's a big misunderstanding out there, that communication is about speaking, presenting, telling, fascinating, convincing. Or, in one verb: pushing.

But that's not what communication is about. People can communicate with silence. Yes, as Paul Watzlawick said, there is no non-communication.[1] There are many different styles of communication. What matters is to know that communication skills are not exclusive to extroverts. Not everybody communicates the same way. Introverts do it differently.

Find your own way of communicating. There is no absolute paradigm, but make sure you don't avoid warm communication, communication in the trustful atmosphere of the below 13 participants and other opportunities to get a mirror and reflect on it.

Seek the feedback of peers, the boss and the team. Don't be afraid of being assessed with a 360-degree tool.

Very important: Use the insight of Myers-Briggs and the tests mentioned in Chapter 3 on 'Enabling' by taking them yourself. I would make them compulsory for everyone groomed to take a management position, before they are considered for one.

Be aware of your language skills. Knowing some words in another language puts your interlocutor at ease in small talk, but don't risk venturing into complex communication in a language you don't master. And if you don't master the preponderant language of your company, either achieve superior knowledge or frankly consider and discuss with your boss what this barrier may really mean for your chances to succeed. It's better to be frank about it than to create misunderstandings that can create damage.

Beware of the 'authenticity trap'. Everybody and their sister-in-law would agree that being authentic is a positive value in management. But very often I've seen that authenticity is used as an excuse to improvise and not be thoroughly prepared for communication with stakeholders. Training is of the utmost importance. The most authentic manager is trained and professional and then he is also honest and true to himself.

Be aware of what you can and can't do

I was once put into a miserable situation. My cell phone rang when I was having a lovely breakfast with a journalist in a Manhattan hotel. It was the CEO's office informing me that I had the disputable honour of being the most senior headquarters' fat cat presently in the United States and that this qualified me to step in for my boss who could not attend a recruitment event at one of the prestigious business schools of that country. I was kindly asked to pack my bag and fly over to the place of the event and present my company and make sure I would make a *bella figura*. We wanted to attract these MBAs to work for us. No presentation in my hands, I boarded the flight and hoped for it to be hijacked by a reggae band and taken to the Caribbean. My time slot was the last of the day and before me the CEO of the most prestigious investment bank and the CEO of the most renowned strategy consulting firm had enthused the audience, winning over all of the young alphas in the auditorium. I had no clue what to say. My self-assessment was quick and crude: odds that I would fail in this task were very high. I had to find a way out that would not hide my lack of competence to comply with the requirement of the situation, while at the same time representing my company well and achieving the goal of the presentation – to attract the best business school students to a German insurance company. And before I let my fears overwhelm me I found courage, breathed briefly and said to myself: 'I am a communicator, not a CEO, they know it, I know it. Let me be what I am and be professional about it.' And I asked the students if they could share a story with me, a story that would be both personal and of societal relevance. Immediately a smartass from the first row raised his hand and said in a slightly annoyed tone, 'This is a typical European question. What exactly do you mean?' I told them a short story. My father (personal) had just been diagnosed with dementia (a societal phenomenon). At that time I was living in Munich, had a brother in Havana, the other brother in Leipzig and my sisters in Rome, while my father lived with his partner in Milan. Which of us siblings would be taking care of our dad and supporting his partner in the task? A girl from the back raised her hand and said that she had lost her parents in a car accident when she was four and was raised by her grandparents. They

▶

were living in a small town in the Midwest, far away from where she would have a career. She felt that the old age care and financial well-being was a challenge she would have to master; it was her time to give back. The next hand was raised by a young man whose parents had just lost their home in Florida after a hurricane. I stopped my little listening exercise here – the examples were just too good to be true. 'Ladies and gentlemen,' I said, 'I understand if you are attracted by the huge boni of an investment bank. If you crave them, help yourself, that's the direction for you. If you want to rule the corporate world by influencing the strategies of many large corporations, follow your instincts and join the strategy consultant. My company provides solutions to both of the problems the lady and the gentleman just mentioned: old age provision and financial protection from natural catastrophes. If you want to do something that makes sense to yourself and to society, come and join us.' I'm not sure if I was able to recruit any of those smart young people. But I did my best, staying both authentic and sticking to my knitting – communicating.

Step 3: Become aware of your context and shape the change to the Listening Leader

If you act as a Listening Leader you will do nothing less than kicking off a change phase. It will be crucial to be fully aware of the environment in which you move. You have to tackle some relevant issues, balance between security and change, checking the cultural awareness of the organisation, pick one of four different change strategies, align the organisation:

1. Find the balance between security and change

'For you to stay healthy, each system in your body and mind must balance two conflicting needs. On the one hand, it must remain open to inputs during ongoing transactions with its local environment; closed systems are dead systems. On the other hand, each system must also preserve a fundamental stability, staying centered around a good set-point and within certain ranges – not too hot, nor too cold.'[2]

The constant feedback from stakeholders is what drives organisational change to higher degrees of excellence. We have an enormous asset, mostly unexploited, as we know: our mind. Our brain is plastic; it's able to adapt to even the most traumatic changes. It has a processing capacity just randomly exploited. Don't be concerned about the amount of things to consider – checklists, golden rules and PowerPoint presentations, whether they are in this book or elsewhere. They are there to help you, to bounce off ideas. Not to be learnt off by heart.

What matters is that you stand firmly on two feet:

- The stability of the values, the strategic framework of the company, the key performance indicators.
- The senses alert to deeply listen to your stakeholders and be able to translate this into the strategy of the company, of your area of responsibility.

In order to manage change, to be agile about learning and adapting, we need a framework that stays pretty much stable. We need both change *and* security.

Where are the areas that should be kept *stable* during times of change?

- **Strategy:** We know that strategy is itself partially stable (the vision and mission of the leader or leaders) *and* flexible (the context, the market). Rather than stable, maybe the right adjective for the security effect of strategy is the recognisability of the strategy in spite of the constant adaptations. A strategy has to be recognisable over a CEO cycle.
- **Vision, mission, purpose:** This basic strategic framework has also got to remain stable. It takes years to enthuse and involve the stakeholders.
- **Values:** Company values in good companies are not decided at the sketchboard. Company values are ideally the result of a complex translation exercise, bottom-up (from the staff to the CEO) and top-down (from the CEO to the employee), but also left-right, right-left, namely with, to and from the stakeholders.

Now that we've seen where some stability has to persist in order not to lose our stakeholders, let's very briefly look at the areas that will never reach a state of stability, at least not from today's economic conditions:

Products, processes, services, information technology and operations, sales, working and collaboration culture.

Don't be bewildered. Yes, all this change is very complex. But this doesn't mean that there is a pre-written solution that allows you to be a good leader in all of those rapidly mutating landscapes. Just keep your senses alert. This is the gist of communicative leadership: develop receptors for your staff, your internal and external customers, your investors and society at large. Smell, touch, taste, watch and listen to changes in society. Stay curious. Be open to adopting these changes because you are also on the safe ground of the vision and values of your company. Use your common sense and you will have a key that opens all doors, especially if you involve your stakeholders. The Listening Leader can tap into many resources.

2. Check the cultural change readiness of your organisation

Is your team or organisation ready for this change? Change readiness can be seen in four areas: inclination, motivation, opportunities and criticism.

Furthermore there are two areas you need to explore – one in *every* change situation, the other related to the particular situation you find yourself in.

- **What to explore in every change.** What are the existing cultures and sub-cultures, the organisation's history and past, how does the team communicate, what are the relationships between management and employees, leadership styles, sense of belonging to the organisation and the level of engagement, existing values (operating and desired), opinion about change and willingness to invest in the project, employee perception?
- **What is specific according to the type of change?** What are the relationships between different organisational sectors (e.g. between headquarters and subsidiaries and branches, the holding company and other group firms, offices and networks etc.), perception regarding challenges (e.g. what could happen if no intervention took place?), organisations and stakeholders (e.g. role and perception of the local organisation, organisational and social relationships, etc.), local and international dimensions as well as relationships which are relevant to the specific change at hand?

3. Pick one of the four change strategies

The change strategy that is to be adopted can vary according to the context and how one wishes to carry out the change. Each of these strategies corresponds to a different interpretation and thus a different way of engaging employees:

- **'Explosive' change management:** An *explosive* approach in terms of both the quantity and visibility of the activity plan. This means an immediate refocusing of your strategy following unexpected changes.
- **'Evolutionary' change management:** An *adaptive* approach in terms of a *gradual* activity plan which values the *adaptive* capacities of people engaged.
- **'Viral' change management:** An approach aimed to *activate the greatest number of people possible*. This is only possible with the engagement of a large number of change agents.
- **'Metamorphic' change management:** An approach aimed to *radically transform the status quo*. This ends with a new beginning, the caterpillar becomes a butterfly.

4. Align the organisation at all employee touch points

Make sure everyone is on board, from your team to your peers to all the stakeholders you interact with. Consistency of behaviours is crucial and once the track has been designed, everyone needs to follow accordingly. To do so, you should cherish Step 4.

Step 4: Do your EMMA work

I already briefly explained the acronym EMMA in the introduction. EMMA should always be in your pocket. It's a simple tool with millions of opportunities for it to be used to improve your personal and corporate communication.

Before every significant interaction you should try to analyse your audience according to EMMA.

- E stands for empathy or expectations of the stakeholders. What do they feel? Where do they stand? What do they expect from you? Put yourself into their shoes.
- M stands for motivation of the stakeholders. What is driving their behaviour, what are their thoughts? Do they want to learn? Are they concerned? Do they want benefits?

- The second M stands for mentality. What do the stakeholders think? Who are they? Age, gender, ethnic background, religion, sexual orientation and many other factors are important to establish a relationship with your stakeholders.
- The A stands for analysis. Make sure you analyse your public before you engage in a dialogue.

Do the obvious: ask

At our corporate university I did role-plays with our managers in order to train effective communication. A typical situation was a town-hall meeting where two different groups acting as C-managers had to both hold a town-hall meeting announcing a restructuring plan. A third group played the staff audience. They all had an hour to prepare and we briefed the two different groups of 'managers' and the remaining group of 'employees'. The employees were briefed on how they should observe the managers in order to vote on the better of the two groups and explain their vote in the feedback session. It was clear to the managers that their performance was assessed by their colleagues in the audience. They had all listened to my previous explanation of EMMA. I don't know how many of those role-plays I've made. In the hour of preparation before the town-hall meeting almost every group tried to analyse expectations, mentality and motivation of the 'staff' audience. In all those years, however, just once a group of 'managers' did the simple thing of walking out of the room, going to the room where the 'staff' were preparing and asking them: 'What do you think? What are your concerns? What are you expecting from this town-hall meeting called with such a short notice?' Needless to say, they performed exceptionally well at the town-hall meeting. One of that group, Gary Bhojwani, later became CEO of an important flagship company and finally an executive board member. Most of the times it's that simple: ask. You can ask one or two of your team members before an important meeting. They will be happy to provide you with this information and you will run a much better meeting, or investors' roadshow, or an event with your distribution partners.

Step 5: Your action plan, a draft

Craft an action plan of what you need to achieve, in line with your organisational objectives and your own role. Don't go for absolutes, remain flexible. This is just a sketch. But what matters is the link to the company strategy of what you do, the connection to the company values. You will have to use this plan every day, to remind yourself and your team of the simple performance indicators that stand for success. So that they can listen and download.

Book yourself a couple of hours in your calendar every quarter. Take out your action plan and ask yourself: what did I hear in the last three months that may make me change this plan? What needs to be escalated to my boss?

Make sure that you achieve a discipline in downloading the input, the complaints and the suggestions for improvement by your stakeholders to those in the company that will benefit from this input. Make sure you regularly consolidate what you and your team have gathered from the stakeholders and share it with your boss. Listening is not an art, it's a discipline.

The CEO's 'working sites'

Michael had just been appointed CEO. He walked into my office with a roll of paper under his arm. 'Let's discuss my strategy,' he said. We had known each other for 10 years, already, and I knew what a structured thinker he is. But I didn't expect him to be that structured. The roll of paper was a huge manifest of A3 pages glued together, a map of the problems of my employer. He called them 'my working sites'. It could have been from Napoleon, except it covered the whole world, while the French dictator and then emperor only wanted to conquer Europe. A true battlefield. With a smirk he said: 'There's a lot from my chief of staff in this …'. It was the perfect draft, not yet a plan. To transform it into the company's strategy, stakeholders needed to be consulted. But it was a strong starting point, opinionated and worth being discussed with those who had an influence on the fate of the company, pretty much in trouble in those days. It was time to check this plan with the stakeholders. It was time to listen.

Step 6: The stakeholder grid

When you start this journey you have a wonderful opportunity to make the right steps from the beginning. After having sketched out a draft plan (Step 5), check the expectations of your stake-holders when starting a new job. Take a sheet of paper and on the left list all the stakeholders you interact with. Your boss, the chair-man should be on this list as well as investors and sell-side ana-lysts, journalists, employees, customers, distributors, regulators and politicians, NGO representatives and the management.

On the right you write some basic questions: what has been good so far? What should change? What needs to be handled urgently and quickly? Which is the major obstacle to better performance? What do you expect from my leadership? What is the most important mistake I should avoid? (See two examples of such a grid in Figures 5.1 and 5.2.)

Arrange meetings with all these stakeholders (including your boss). You can even start before the new job commences. But by 100 days after your appointment you should have personally met all the stakeholders you had identified.

By doing so you achieve a couple of results:

1. You *get the EMMA* of your stakeholders.

2. You get to *know* your stakeholders.

3. You *position yourself as a Listening Leader*, because the first con-tact is not barking orders but asking good questions.

4. *They get to know you* very quickly.

5. You can *adapt your strategy* to the input of the stakeholders and improve it. This occurs by taking out your action plan (see Step 5) and matching it with the input of the stakeholders. Does it still stand? Does it have to be changed?

There is a final advantage to using this grid: you gain time.

What happens usually?

A freshly appointed manager would wait to meet the stakeholders until he has something to say about what he intends to do. Since finding out what to do always consumes time, you normally don't see the stakeholders for a longer period before you dare tackle them with your action plan. While you do your homework time passes and they will think that you've forgotten them: 'He's been in his new job six weeks now and he hasn't come to see me!'

Figure 5.1 Emilio's grid for line managers (exemplary)

STAKEHOLDER	QUESTIONS					
	What can we do better in order to support the strategy?	What do you expect from me and my team?	How can we help you to succeed?	Where should the team improve?	Where are we from 0–10?	What should we do to reach 10?
My boss						
My peers						
My customers a) internal b) external						
My suppliers						
Corporate communications on: • media • GOs and NGOs • strategy • blogosphere/social media						
HR off: • development/training • workplace flexibility						
Selection: • customers • complaints						
Investor relations • investors						
Compliance						
Millennials						
Old hands						

Figure 5.2 Emilio's grid for CEOs (exemplary)

STAKEHOLDER	QUESTIONS					
	What should I keep?	What should I change now?	Main obstacles to success	Potentials we need to better exploit	Where are we from 0–10?	What should we do to reach 10?
Chairperson						
C-suite colleagues						
Rank and file staff						
Interns/millennials						
Sell-side analysts						
Journalists						
Regulators						
Government						
Opposition parties						
Relevant NGOs						
Bloggers (relevant)						
Neighbours (in manufacturing)						
Sales people						
Distribution partners						
Consumerist associations						

If you meet them soon after starting the new job you establish a quick contact ('One day in his office and he already convened a staff meeting and met the two most important customers, what a wonderful person!') without the need to make any commitment since you just started. Maybe it is too soon for you to say something, but it's not too soon to listen to the other person. To be ready to step into action mode.

Step 7: Start!

If you truly communicate it will allow you to try and fail and correct very quickly. So, get started! One of the big mistakes of change is to try to be on the safe side and figure out how exactly things have to be in the new world. Before you start, you may want to be 100 per cent sure. The journey is long and you will make lots of mistakes, that's natural. But if you truly communicate you may be able to pre-empt most mistakes, warned by your stakeholders. Since this journey will be long, you better start now.

When you have started, you will have kicked off a change process, involving yourself, your team and all the other stakeholders. Years of good practice in change management have taught us how to deal with these issues. As chairman of Methodos S.p.A., the Change Management Company, I'm sitting on numerous vaults containing the jewels of almost four decades of experience. Too much for a book.

So my company has drilled them down to ten rules – five things to do and five to avoid.

The big five of today's change management

1. **Share a collective dream** of a change vision (i.e. to become a digital company) with the top management and spread it throughout your team and the organisation.

2. **Walk the talk:** involve all other leaders from the start and enable them to visibly direct the change.

3. **Engage people across the board:** involve the whole organisation in working towards the vision. Change will not occur if culture and behaviours are not consistent at all levels.

4. **Consider all company stakeholders from a social media perspective:** plan a stakeholder governance strategy that engages relevant stakeholders both inside and outside the company.

5. **Develop a change dashboard** to monitor and lead the change; leading and lagging KPIs serve to show the value created for different stakeholders and to redirect the change process according to achieved results.

There are frequent roadblocks to change; this is natural. Not everybody embraces change and for many the trade-off between change and security can turn out to be unfavourable. They lose too much stability in the process and need to decide whether to adapt or to look for another job.

There are five very frequent mistakes that, one by one, can jeopardise a change process. So, try to avoid them.

The five most common mistakes of change management

1. **Maintaining old habits and behaviours:** resistance to change can be mapped and should be managed. Identify the pockets of resistance and try to understand them but act swiftly to remove old habits and behaviours that block the transformation. Losing time on committing this mistake will lead to cynicism and the loss of support for the change programme ('nothing really happens, there is no change').

2. **Focusing only on digital and technological needs:** it is the world that is changing and the whole team must evolve in order to lead rather than follow change. Change encompasses all of our lives and technology impacts social habits and labour relations. But demographic change, healthcare, life expectancy, diverse thought patterns between generations and diversity at large: they do influence change as well and need to be considered, not only the smartphone and social media.

3. **An 'everybody should definitely change! ... except for me'** **attitude:** do not allow room for exceptions in the adoption of new behaviours. It starts with you. Be consistent and always be an example. It is much easier to drive change if you can lead

by example – there can be no excuses if the manager becomes a consistent leader.

4. **Neglecting the human factor:** culture is a fundamental asset of change and it is key to making a change successful. Interfaces cannot replace personal relations and people engagement. Trust is the grease that makes the clockwork function and trust is not created by an algorithm. Yet.

5. **Declaring change as accomplished:** change is not an event, it is a journey. Changing mindsets and behaviours both inside and outside the company is a considerable undertaking. Ongoing support activities are essential to guarantee an effective change. Therefore never promise a land of milk and honey. It might come, but the train won't stop there, it will move on to the next station Which may well be in the desert.

Every defeat is a victory

Andreotto, my now retired brother-in-law, had a happy-go-lucky attitude towards setbacks in his job. He always used to say 'Every defeat is a victory.' I never really understood what he meant and tried to make a sense of it. And to try out whether he was right or not.

Imagine you want a budget increase for your department in times of cost-cutting. You know you'll never get it, your boss will say 'no', so you better not ask from the beginning. Wrong. Ask, justify why you think it would be good for the company. Listen to your boss's explanations of why it doesn't work. Acknowledge the 'no' with your supervisor, accept the defeat and get on with your life.

Next time you have something to ask, do it again, don't self-censor. Get the next explicit 'no', acknowledge the next defeat.

If you are a good performer, your boss will be sitting on thorns next time you ask for something making business sense. Probably, the third time there will be a 'yes' and you can see that the previous defeats brought you this victory. It may be a much more important decision than just a budget increase.

Had you censored yourself not asking the first two times, you would be at square one every time you wish to achieve something.

You may encounter obstacles on your communicative leadership journey. Don't lose patience even in case of a setback. A Listening Leader has to be resilient, that journey is long. And failing is an edge on the others. Don't forget what Thomas Edison said, when confronted with many failures during his career as an inventor: 'I have not failed. I've just found 10,000 ways that won't work.' With more than 1,000 patented inventions he is the most prolific inventor known so far.

So, actively look for scars on the battlefield. Dare. Dare to lose some battles to win the war of the enthusiasm of your stakeholders.

A leader in action needs energy – where to get it from

Time to think: Companies are full of *Alice in Wonderland's* White Rabbits rushing around with their watches in their hand. An often-heard remark is: 'If I only had the time to think, I'm just so busy getting things done …'. I've been there. I made this mistake more often than I would like to admit.

Time invested in thinking is time saved mending a crisis. Time invested in thoroughly building the proper strategy, with clear and understandable key performance indicators, with achievable *and* stretched goals, time devoted to establishing the brand attributes and declining them to company values and desired behaviours is time you gain further down the process.

A sound – well *thought*-through – strategic framework allows all the empowered employees of a listening company to act as entrepreneurs. If they only act as entrepreneurs without a clear strategic frame chaos will ensue. If they have a sound strategic setup but are neither well informed, nor listening to stakeholders, unable to build the skillset and knowledge necessary to work well and are not empowered to shape the company's fate, the company will lose its license to operate (to build a superior thinking environment read *Time to Think* by Nancy Kline).

Time to think in action

Claudia Danser, a friend, my former tutorial partner in the Meyler Campbell Business Coaching Programme and one of the rising stars of coaching saw the power of Nancy Kline's gospel and how important it is to find time to think. She coaches Dermot.

Dermot is a brilliant, charismatic and hard-working director at The Prince's Trust. As part of our coaching, Dermot wanted to understand how others perceived him and how he could be a better leader. The 360-degree feedback I collated for him strongly reinforced what he suspected – he really needed to listen more, give his team more space and time in order to develop and fully motivate them. It turned out that this might also be blocking his own promotion in the company. If he could manage to empower his team more, he'd also benefit from a lighter workload as he was near exhaustion from doing everything himself. Inspired, Dermot decided to do a number of things to truly empower his team. One idea was to run an event where he invited the level below his direct reports to spend an afternoon with him to think about how best to achieve the organisation's growth plans. Up until then, he had almost always come up with the ideas himself but he appreciated that great, well-informed ideas could also come from those who worked more closely day to day with the young people the charity supports. Using the attention, listening and questions from Nancy Kline's *Time to Think*, Dermot ran the event. Instead of the usual leader 'transmit' mode, he listened. The junior team shared, he listened, he didn't interrupt. They shared some more. He listened. And by the end of the event, they had generated so many useful and important new ideas that their thoughts ended up being translated into the headline objectives for the region's new business plan. The additional benefit was that the junior members of Dermot's team felt so much more involved, motivated and engaged. Not only had Dermot seen brilliant results from empowering his team, he had also gained a wonderful insight into his stakeholders – both the up-and-coming stars in his department (so he could better succession plan) and the young people that The Prince's Trust supports. Due to its success, Dermot repeated the event and continues to empower his team, organising a day for this junior group to discuss their ideas and engage directly with the Trust's CEO and wider senior management team for the benefit of the whole organisation.

You need both: a listening organisation within a sound strategic frame.

The CEO is paid to advance this agenda but you as a line manager are co-responsible for the fate of the organisation and you can improve your own performance and the license to operate of your own team. Give yourself the time for it.

Be clear, to all. What matters is making the change agenda transparent – to all stakeholders. Create clarity around why listening is so important for a better performance and that this allows stakeholders to own their share of the company and help to shape it into a fitter body. A body delivering superior products that enthuse the customer and thereby initiate the virtuous circle of profitable growth: an enthusiastic customer will recommend the company. This will make the company grow profitably, attracting investors. A stronger company can hire and groom the best talents and provide them with the motivation that stems from being empowered, to make a difference, including the lady at the reception desk, our Director of First Impressions.

These stakeholders will stand up for the company and they will grant it the license to successfully operate as an accepted corporate citizen.

Have a dashboard. Every leader and every company embarking on this journey is well-advised to take a snapshot of where it stands at the beginning of the change. What is the *engagement* of the employees? How strong is the recommendation will of customers (*NPS*)? What is the *financial performance* of the company? How does it score in *sustainability indices*?

The change dashboard should be updated regularly. But don't make it an encyclopaedic exercise. One KPI per stakeholder is enough to provide a proper framework that allows for entrepreneurial action and the adaptation of the strategy according to the changing context, market, environment. I have seen companies blocked by the abundance of KPIs, sometimes even apparently contradicting each other (two charts on the Methodos Dashboard).

Celebration times come on!

I don't tend to cry much over spilled milk. But at this point I have to confess to one of my many mistakes, important enough to be mentioned.

It was the second year in a row that my Munich department had given me the satisfaction of a remarkably good engagement survey. There was just one disturbing detail. In our survey there was a question I actually always wondered about. 'Did you celebrate your successes?' For two years in a row my staff gave its leadership pretty bad marks. It referred to the whole management team in my area, but who was leading them? Me. So it was a message to me.

This question irritated me. Are we here to perform a job, reach our goals and do our duty or are we a partying organisation? What does 'celebrate' mean? Some hypocritical event, a Christmas party, to pat ourselves on the back, being careful not to let the champagne glass spill any of the precious bubbly on the person we pat? My God, it took me a few of just those events to understand that I was so wrong. My team didn't want a cocktail party. They didn't even necessarily want an event. They wanted recognition. They wanted a moment of pause to absorb the good outcome of a project, to recognise the common efforts and the individual contributions. Nothing more. But since I didn't get it the first time, they sent me a strong message the year after in the next engagement survey. The penny dropped. How much time did I waste without fully recognising the contributions of the team and its members instead of taking the time to do so and enhance motivation and thereby performance?

Hold your breath and savour the moment

What really matters in terms of recognition is the awareness and the ability to feel that moment.

Here are two of the points neurologist Richard Hanson suggests for the individual and that fit a Listening Leader (excerpts):

1. Turn positive facts into positive experiences. Good things keep happening all around us, but much of the time we don't notice them; even when we do, we often hardly feel them. [...] Whatever

positive facts you find, bring a mindful awareness to them – open up to them and let them affect you. It's like sitting down at a banquet: don't just look at it – dig in!

2. Savour the experience. [...] You could strengthen your feelings of satisfaction after completing a demanding project by thinking about some of the challenges you had to overcome.[3]

So, it's not about having parties in the office, all the time. Simply be aware of the efforts and achievements of yourself and your team. Acknowledge them, stand still with your team and savour the moment. It can be at a normal staff meeting or you may even hold one especially for the occasion.

Yes, they're all being paid to work, but the salary doesn't include the energy, enthusiasm, self-motivation and team spirit that are needed to succeed. Honour this and you will be honoured.

On stress and work–life integration

'Difficult states of mind, including stress, low mood, distractibility, relationship issues, anxiety, sorrow, and anger.'[4] These are all consequences of stress.

All of this may also be what lies between a willing person *wanting* to become a Listening Leader and actually *being* one.

The consequences of stress are lack of concentration, bad sleep, the constant feeling of running behind time: the symptoms of a modern manager under strain. At the beginning of this book I promised communicative leadership would put you ahead of events, allowing you to shape the agenda of your working life instead of being moulded by it.

This is especially needed in times of continuous alarm mode, 24/7/365, with stakeholders armed with a smartphone that can turn into a global medium in a second.

Paradoxically, it's not by accelerating your life that you get in front of events, it's by pausing, regularly.

Please, don't say, 'Oh, it's about the work–life balance!' It's not. Actually this expression is misleading as such. Why should there be an antagonism between work and life? Isn't work part of our life?

I believe that to lead a balanced life you need to earn your living by loving what you do. Otherwise, prepare for change: read Herminia Ibarra's highly inspiring *Working Identity*[5] and reinvent your career.

And maybe take a minute to ponder the views of a millennial on work–life integration. We may learn from it.

Work–life integration – what's the fuss about? A millennial's view

Work-related stress is now recognised as one of the biggest health issues of our century. It can have devastating effects on the individual. Heightened blood pressure and levels of adrenaline, when occurring over a long period of time, can lead to heart problems and other related maladies. Psychologically, stress can cause emotional exhaustion and even burnout. Besides, productivity is lowered as a result, too.

In an effort to avoid these outcomes, it is important to take time out from work. Breaks at work, sufficient sleep, physical activity, weekends and holidays are all great contributors to the physical and mental recovery from work.

This is why I am highly sceptical of the now so popular 'work is your home' model of many companies of Silicon Valley (but not only). While it sounds fantastic to be able to play games, have your hair done or even nap at work, a little nagging feeling I have is that employees are being lured into a 24-hour commitment to their work and companies. This sounds oddly familiar: friends tell me that some offices in big law firms or financial institutions are equipped with beds for those who might have to stay the night to work through a project. The reward for this is usually a big pay cheque, career progression and the prestige of these companies plays a big role in the lure. But is it worth it? Definitely not on the same scale but still of relevance is the reminder that, a century ago, when women weren't allowed to vote and slaves existed in our society, the slaves would be housed and fed in order to allow the master control over working times and other conditions of their working life. With a critical eye towards inappropriate comparisons and an acknowledgment of the historical and cultural context, is there still a justifiable opinion that we voluntarily hand over the reins of our lives to these companies? I believe we should think a little bit about what we are actually giving up when blinded by the shiny goodies they dangle in front of our eyes.

Apart from switching off away from work, one of the most highly determining factors in one's well-being in this context is how well one's work fits in with one's personal beliefs, needs, passions and talents.

The biggest misunderstanding around the term work–life balance (and the reason for its replacement with new term work–life integration) is that work and life should be so separated and removed that people work in a job they hate in order to fund what their real passion is. This will make the employee unhappy, both at work and not (just consider that the time spent working constitutes the biggest chunk of the waking day). It will also hinder productivity, creativity and career development, all of which have an impact on both the employee, the team, the work climate and the company.

In order for employees to thrive, they must align their career choices with their interests, goals and strengths.

Ever more so than before, the Y generation is looking for work to be in sync with the personal value system. With the wide array of choices available to us, we are reluctant to settle for a job or a company we don't trust or don't approve of. This generation cares about equality, the environment, civil and human rights, among other things. Since we are the employees and customers of the future and already of significant importance now, smart companies better start thinking where they stand on such issues and what type of individual they are attracting as a result.

Furthermore, our generation, in comparison to previous ones, where being junior meant accepting non-recognised extra work, feel entitled to challenge this order and leave the office at 5pm. Of course, this is too extreme and especially we, who ask for flexibility, should be ready to put in extra effort and time where necessary. And I believe that many of us do when the work we do means something to us. While previously people might have reluctantly stayed in the office for a job they hated, because of their perception of work as a chore, young people today want more out of a job, and when that need is fulfilled, they, too, give their jobs a big chunk of themselves, their time and their effort.

Legal drug: Why not try mindfulness and meditation?

There are natural steroids that can help you boost your performance, deal with stress having no headache the next morning or any other dangerous addiction. Actually, more than steroids it's directly about hormones, endorphins, dopamines. It's about the conscious ability to stimulate your brain.

If you already love your work but want to improve the fun, reduce the stress, increase your performance and thereby find more time for the other things in life, you might want to consider meditation.

I've come across some impressive personalities in management. Most of them had their own recipe: many of them fitness, some of them yoga, tai-chi, other chess-playing or playing an instrument. A very busy CEO I know plays the violin every day he's at home.

For the masters of alibis ('I just can't do this, because …'), pretending not to have time for daily fitness, to have ligament problems that don't allow them to practise yoga, that their neighbours would laugh at them if they practised tai-chi ('So, what?' I would say) and that learning an instrument is just too time consuming, I have a suggestion that doesn't allow for excuses. Or tell me you wouldn't have 20 minutes in the morning and 20 minutes in the evening to meditate?

Believe me, it pays off. I have practised meditation since 2011. Mindfulness, or, if you want more traditional terms, focus and concentration highly benefit from regular meditation. If you don't take my word for it, if you decide to ignore hundreds of years of contemplative practices in Buddhism, Christianity, Islam, Hinduism and Judaism – all of which have their version of ascetism – then you may want to lend your ear to a neurologist and a neuropsychologist and read *Buddha's Brain*. You will find an impressive amount of information on how our brain helps to shape the mind and how meditation helps to reach happiness and wisdom, analysing how exactly our brain with its different parts can be trained and stimulated to improve performance.

You are at the end of the journey to communicative leadership. You have now earned the black belt of the Listening Leader.

And now let's do the 'millennial' check on their expectations towards the black-belt-wearing Listening Leader.

Reverse mentoring – the babyboomer asks the millennial about their Expectations Motivations Mentality Analysis (EMMA)

Mentoring is shifting towards being a two-way street. The following debate is an illustration of such reverse mentoring. In the name of the old world, companies and leaders at his level, Emilio asks Clementina for her and her peers' perspective on leadership and companies today and in the future. Clementina has communicated with and challenged communities of millennials in Europe, but takes full responsibility for her choice of answers.

What do you expect from us as leaders and the team?

From the Listening Leader we expect:

1. **An ethical vision** of the world and where the company fits into the social and environmental well-being of the communities at stake. We want to have clear messages on where the company stands in respect to:

   - integrity
   - respect of work–life integration
   - equal treatment and opportunities independent of age, gender and so forth.

2. **Inspiration:** The leader should be able to organise the idea-gathering by the team, foster the ability to connect different networks of relationships and stakeholders from science to virtual communities, to connect and cross-fertilise the team, in other words accompany what we now know as being one of the premier products of our brain and its neuronal network and the synaptic connections.

3. **Guidance:** The leader should master the basic managerial skills and be able to set the frame for the work, creative and less so. A leader has to have the proper project management skills, be able to manage by objectives and set the stage for the staff to work as independently as the structures allow. We are an annoyingly indecisive bunch, so we will look for reassurance and guidance from you where needed.

4. **Role model:** The leader should be consistent with the vision and the strategy and be a role model for the values of the company. Walk the talk.

5. **Fearless developer:** The leader should not be scared of developing people and letting them grow.

6. **Driver of change:** The ability to also push against the past will earn a leader the support of the millennials.

7. **Become digital:** The leaders should be open to new technology and media and become able to use them autonomously and flexibly and to interact with the staff. What should not happen is to have a leader resisting technological change and delegating it to the younger workforce staying in his old-world trench.

8. **StrengthsFinder:** Able to create and manage a team leveraging the strengths of each team member.

9. **Curious people person:** Ask us and listen to us and to all other team members irrespective of their age or any other criterion about how we can contribute to the company's success with innovative and fresh ideas.

10. **Proactive empathy:** Understand that there may be barriers, such as shyness or social clumsiness, and make it easier for us to open up to the personal circumstances that may negatively affect our performance. Create an atmosphere of trust and proactively seek an open exchange.

Expected impact of the Listening Leader on teams:

1. **Informal (almost friendly) relationships:** Allow people to feel at ease with each other.

2. **Respect:** Create a positive climate of collaboration and mutual respect; don't stir artificial internal competition within a team:

listening and support of each other is the way to boost the team's performance.

3. **Diversity:** Build a heterogeneous team, with different competences, professions, life experiences and with a multicultured mindset. Leverage on those differences in order to gain more holistic views or to discover new angles.

4. **Open:** The team should be able to be transparent and honest in the relationships and open about discussing its dynamics.

Where are we on the way to meeting millennials' expectations by employers? A very personal assessment from 1–10.

1. UK – big firms: 5; small and medium sized: 6

2. Italy – big firms: 4; small and medium sized: 3

3. Germany – 5

4. France – 4

5. Benelux – 6

6. USA – 3 (on work–life integration); 7 (enabling and empowerment)

What should leaders and companies do to reach 10?

To gain our unconditional buy-in, companies should have a clear purpose and everything and everybody in the company should be aligned towards pursuing this purpose. The development money should be put where the strategy mouth is. For example, don't claim to be a company with a global scope if you don't have real international career opportunities.

One of the most important vectors of this pursuit is the enablement of dynamic exchange through breaking down hierarchical and physical barriers (e.g. open door policy, connection and integration with the academic world). It should be the norm for leaders to involve people, to tap into their ideas and skills in order to let them co-own the company, the results, the project. They should listen, but also actively ask their employees about their strengths, weaknesses, frustrations, improvements, dreams, needs, circumstances. Long-term challenges in HR practice should also be addressed. An example is the enablement of flexibly portable old-age provision across borders and employers.

Different cultures, backgrounds, mindsets, personalities should be accommodated. This effort should be reflected first and foremost in recruitment selection criteria, to allow for non-standard job profiles. Anglo-Saxon countries are leading this development, while countries like Italy, Germany and France are still very formal on the 'optimal' education and career paths of candidates.

Companies and leaders should honour the commitment to improving work–life integration. Finally, in order to be trustworthy and credible in their pursuit of meritocracy, there should be more transparency on pay slots and clear career paths.

What are the most important established business practices that we should keep?

One of the attitudes of millennials, which, in a different form, has always been present, is a respectful attitude towards leaders. There should be no fear of the leader, a reaction more traditionally linked with respect of seniority. However, millennials believe that Listening Leaders have earned the right to be fully respected. At the same time, leaders should keep taking responsibility for their actions, something that should be extended to everybody within the company through further empowerment.

Millennials are also still interested in certain elements of the incentive system. They welcome options of co-ownership, equity participation, management buy-out options. They are also seduced by fringe benefits, albeit a reloaded version. Rather than money and luxury, fringe benefits by employers should look at welfare (e.g. old age provision) and ease of life (e.g. nursery and child-care, home office, transport facilitations). Additionally, in line with current trends, they would like the evaluation of more than just financial aspects to be reinforced.

One final fundamental business practice to keep and aspire to is stakeholder engagement and the striving for win-win solutions.

What should companies change now to be attractive to millennials?

To attract young talents, companies ought to leave behind fears of losing power or status and nurture a culture of autonomy and flexibility, as this is much more important to millennials than job security, which is the reason they might leave you if they don't find the characteristics of this culture in your organisation. In order to foster such a mindset, companies should also physically create open, informal, transparent and smart work environments and spaces (e.g. open space offices rather than usual closed offices).

We are attracted to companies in which meritocratic growth processes and systems, based upon goals and results, are reported on. The commitment to diversity of all kinds must be leading the company towards a near future in which this topic does not have to be an issue anymore.

What mistakes do we need to avoid, especially when recruiting millennials?

1. **Lack of integrity:** Misalignment between a company's reputation, what the firm wants to portray itself as and what the reality is.

2. **Overly traditional structures:** Old hierarchical conservative company cultures as well as bureaucratisation and slow executives, taking ages to decide and not making their decision-making process transparent are hurdles in the way of a unified workforce and company.

3. **Wrong management appointments:** A bad boss creates havoc and puts a break on all the energy.

4. **Short-term focus:** We want to build something, we don't want to become your Alice in Wonderland Rabbit hastening from quarterly report to quarterly report.

5. **Blind empowering:** Empowering without first making sure there is a sense of psychological safety (exuded by leader), so people can make mistakes, admit them and move on, rather than running around like loose chickens, everybody for themselves, scared of admitting insecurities of failures and therefore stunned subsequent improvement.

6. **Lack of attention towards social and environmental issues.**

7. **Politics and complexity in relationships:** Being respectful and gentle shouldn't be superficial and actually hiding a culture in

which our interactions within the company are managed only according to politics, power-games, unwritten rules and hidden fraternities.

8. **Idealisation of categories** (e.g. stereotypes, expectations, etc.): One example is the millennial categorisation (as opposed to being senior). Ironically, one of the stereotypes of millennials is that of being individualistic. Wanting to be seen for what we are as a person is what matters. The sense of belonging to one single community only is totally strange to our way of thinking. It's just a useless and time-consuming effort to stick us into a specific drawer: environmentalist, fitness-freak, intellectual.

9. **Brainwashing:** Creating an overwhelmingly homogeneous culture with the touch and feel of a slightly value-twisting and manipulating culture. The company may well suggest values that help achieve a corporate vision but that doesn't mean that the company tells us what's right and what's wrong when it comes to personal choice and value-sets within the frame of a democratic society.

How can we help you to succeed?

1. **Give us a chance and don't fear our autonomy:** Autonomy shouldn't mean being removed from the specific project goals or wider business objectives. It should mean a culture in which everybody is free to structure their own work flow and where unnecessary structures simply fall away and the necessary ones remain. Once the aims and expectations are agreed upon, and open and frequent communication possibilities are established, leave us to it and we will do our best to deliver according to how we work best.

2. **Become able to admit and accept our mistakes:** We will make mistakes, especially when new to an organisation. But let's work together to learn from them. Is the mistake grounded in a wrong approach, lack of skills, skewed expectations or misunderstanding? Something else completely? We are hungry to learn about ourselves and improve our shortcomings. In order not to waste this opportunity for both parties, we must be honest about the mistakes and would love a little of your time and expertise to turn mistakes into learnings.

3. **Be a coaching leader.**

4. **Support our development:** We'll walk the extra mile for the company. But we would love to be able to grow in the process. We mean opportunities for professional and personal growth, professional education, access to courses, conferences, lectures, staff exchanges and so forth, with **personalised development plans** for the long term (hereby also showing the employee the company's long-term investment in the person).

5. **Engage us, involve us in organisational actions and decisions:** We are aware that our voices may not count for much in a big organisation and are not disillusioned that we have all the answers, but we live in times in which individuals have been able to shake things up for the better through being given a platform to air their thoughts and ideas.

6. **Constantly challenge us, within the realm of the achievable:** It can be great for us as we can discover our own strengths and talents, as well as our limits. New challenges are a sure-fire way to counteract the trend of high job mobility so characteristic of this generation.

7. **Reward us based on what we deliver:** To millennials there are two sides of the coin here. On the one hand, many of us have gone through internships after internships without seeing a contract, monetary remuneration or reference letter (and the fact that we whine about it may entitle you to call us spoilt brats). On the other hand, today's increasingly permissive and soft society has meant that we have been overly praised for performing averagely. Let's find a middle ground that is fair. When we deliver effort and results, reward us – either financially or with opportunities for growth.

8. **Provide us with feedback:** Being young and energised, just like previous generations, we have the ambition to learn and work hard. However, today, differently from previous times, constructive criticism is the norm and the mantra of 'Just get on with it!' is no longer so widely accepted socially. Targeted, immediate feedback after a task has a much more concrete feel and impact than annual reviews, as time can cloud the memories of both the person evaluating performance and the person

who carried out the task. So really, it's a win-win if feedback is concrete and timely.

What are the potentials we need to exploit (and aren't exploiting thus far)?

The first potential of millennials that comes to mind is techno-logical savviness. Of course, young people have the highest levels of skills in this realm, as they are digital natives, but they can also help unlock the huge potential for this area in babyboomers. We should enable older people in organisations by reverting roles: the millennial becomes the digital mentor to the digitally underdeveloped babyboomer mentee.

Secondly, millennials bring with them an entrepreneurial, inno-vative and creative spirit, partly nurtured through wider global exposure to topics, people and mindsets through social and digi-tal media. It does not necessarily involve artistic creativity, but revolves around problem-solving and the inception and develop-ment of original ideas. We prefer to ask how to make ideas come true rather than explaining why an idea might never succeed. Leverage our diversity and unconventional perspective to jointly shape the future. We can also utilise our global connected net-work to build communities, to help organise the input by stake-holders, to discuss dilemmas in global communities.

What really resonates with you, particularly relevant for you as a millennial?

Beyond everything else, the concept that mostly resonates with us is caring. Caring for each other, for all the stakeholders, for the values and principles the company stands for. Caring about the different responsibilities towards communities and interest groups, about integrity. Profit should be a secondary goal to the objective of caring.

6

Chapter

Conclusion: How to re-establish the lost trust in leadership and succeed as a leader and as a corporation

It was a chilly winter morning in Munich and my mood was in keeping with the outside temperature when I walked down the corridor leading to my office. A phone was ringing in one of the offices in my department. It kept ringing and ringing until I finally reached Frank's office, the editor of our employee magazine. I rushed into the room and answered his phone. It was an elderly lady, married to a pensioner of my company. Like all the other retired colleagues he received our employee magazine regularly. The lady informed me that her husband was terminally ill and would pass away in the near future. She wanted to cancel the subscription to the magazine. I took down her husband's name and address and while doing so a thought crossed my mind: 'These Germans are really different from us Italians. Her husband is dying and she is ticking boxes off a list like an efficient manager.' I had just lost my mother and I could empathise with her situation. I wished her some good last moments with her husband. Then I told her that a more important question would come up in the inevitable moment of her husband's passing: she was entitled to a widow's pension and I knew that quite some paperwork would be necessary to get her pension and not all of it was self-explanatory, especially for a person grieving and with her mind occupied with many other things to be addressed after such a loss. So I gave her the name and extension number of a very nice colleague in charge of those pensions who I was sure would help her tackle pending issues. I bade her goodbye and pensively put

▶

down the phone. Suddenly I noted that there had been someone sitting in Frank's room, waiting for him. It was Nils, a corporate communications colleague from a subsidiary company. My foul mood that icy morning, the strange call I took and the embarrassed expression on Nils' face made me explode: 'Why the hell didn't you take the call? Didn't you hear the phone ringing a dozen times? Have you ever heard of customer focus?' Probably I shot another half a dozen of questions at him and the tone of my voice was clearly not amused. Nils stammered something like: 'But it wasn't my phone …' to which I barked back 'Do you think it was mine? But I took the call!' He then mumbled that he wouldn't have known what to say, that he was not working for the holding company but just for a subsidiary and wasn't sure whether he would trespass rules by answering the phone and saying something wrong. I fumed that there can't be a big margin of error in taking down a call and left the room so as not to further humiliate this useless bozo.

I must have told this story dozens of times to illustrate what a proper attitude towards customer focus should be, that every person getting in touch with an employee is to be considered a customer and treated with respect and best-in-class service. Nils was the perfect example of ineptitude. The only merciful thing I did was to change his name in telling this true story.

Now is the moment to apologise to Nils. It took me a summer break and a sudden thought in my country house remembering that scene, to realise how wrong and unfair I had been with him. Especially how I didn't listen to what he said and what this story said about our organisation. Nils said he wouldn't know what to say. What he meant: he was not enabled to act on behalf of his colleague. Nils also said he was not working for the holding company and wasn't sure whether he would trespass any rules. What he meant: he was not empowered. So, it may well be that this story was a good example of lack of customer focus. In fact, it was a much better story about a leader who didn't listen – me – and an organisation that was so hierarchical that it scared people off taking up responsibility.

I'm sorry, Nils. I owe you my apologies and I also owe you the breakthrough to communicative leadership. My horizons were limited by all my efforts to reach a first-class communication at my company. I hadn't noticed that there was more to it than good communication and that I personally needed to become a better leader and do my best to push the company I worked for into the direction of communicative leadership.

My unfair judgement of Nils and what I learnt from this story prompted me to write this book on that journey I myself travelled in my corporate time.

Whatever we achieved there was the result of many very intelligent people with a very sound value set.

But *how* did we achieve some success on that journey? How did we manage to enrol so many colleagues to advance a corporate agenda for which I had no explicit mandate by the company except for the commitment to train managers to better communicate and make the corporate communicators more business-savvy?

The answer sounds too simple to be true: because it makes sense to listen to stakeholders and use their input to adapt the strategy of the company. It makes business sense. It can be explained to anyone and practised by everyone.

The huge advantage we had was the awareness by our top management that there was a greater good than our individual shining in the spotlights: being accepted by society, being awarded the license to operate.

In hindsight I think much of this was due to the industry I worked in, insurance. Insurance people know that the industry has a rather lousy reputation in most of the markets, that legal thrillers normally place Mr Evil in a rich insurance company with deep pockets, legions of lawyers and that this insurer will crunch every resistance with money and paragraphs.

Add to this that insurance matters are not a typically pleasant subject of conversation with your partner at breakfast. It's evil, even if it's a necessary evil, as everyone understands.

Probably this helped. Because, believe it or not, insurance people are human beings. I know, this is a hazardous hypothesis, but bear with me for a minute. Let's just postulate insurance people are humans with families, friends, neighbours and that even though they work for evil they are embedded in a social context.

Making the difference for our customers and enthusing them was an opportunity to score points that would make us be accepted by our environment. The company had undergone rough times in 2005 and 2006 for somewhat clumsily managing a restructuring process that was urgent and necessary and whose necessity was understood by everyone, including the trade unions that organised demos in front of our head office.

The *way* we had implemented this restructuring was questioned by our stakeholders. Not in terms of facts and figures and productivity goals and simplification of a byzantine structure we had before. That was fine. All of this was understood by employees, customers, investors.

A lost opportunity to listen

To do our restructuring we needed to negotiate all the details with the unions. But first we needed to come up with a plan. The plan was due after nine months, an eternity. This company had months of uncertainty, no answers to the many questions of our staff in that country. It was a nightmare for our local managers. The employees would ask their team leader what would happen to them. The team leader wouldn't know and would in turn ask his department head and so forth up the line onto the country head who would ask for patience since the working groups tasked with planning the new set-up would have to do their homework first, helped by management consultants of a very renowned firm.

The situation was truly difficult and we suffered from the heavy blows to our reputation in that country.

Since everybody pointed at the management consultancy we called a meeting with those consultants. We were sitting in front of half a dozen eggheads with an average IQ that was three times mine. They summed up the situation and illustrated their working hypothesis and why there wouldn't be any chance to have exact figures on staff redundancies before June.

We asked how they thought we should be communicating from now on – four months had passed by now. I also told them how our managers told us they were losing all their credibility and respect when every day they would have to shrug their shoulders to questions by concerned staff members. They looked at me as if I was an alien. And they looked at my boss to detect body language that would allow them to ignore or belittle my question. My boss stuck to me and didn't blink. They were puzzled by my question. 'We have just tried to explain that there is nothing to be communicated before the nine months are over.'

By now you have understood what had happened and where the misunderstanding lay. The management consultants had mistaken information for communication. While the sketchboard analysts with their high IQ were scheming new structures and reckoning headcounts and synergies, those who had most of the answers were not asked. And I should have done something about it. It was my failure.

The months between the announcement of the restructuring and the nine months necessary to negotiate with the unions could have been used to have a bottom-up and a left-and-right picture by the organisation: where can we save? Which processes can be simplified? Where do we duplicate work, where is there too much bureaucracy?

I'm not belittling the gargantuan effort by the consultants and all those involved in the projects. I'm just stating that this experience taught me the lesson that you better listen to stakeholders. Of course the staff wouldn't necessarily have come up with the perfect solution, but their input would have been precious.

Precious it was, as the leaders of that company showed some years later, correcting some of the flaws of the new structure – mainly correcting how to lead.

Take courage!

I would like to encourage managers to take responsibility for their customers and employees and kick off a process that has all the potential to become contagious in your company and likely to be followed by others. Word of mouth will spread. Engagement surveys will confirm this effort. Communicative leadership can be tackled by everyone, from the team manager to the head of larger units.

I would also tell CEOs: Dare, you can only win. Become a courageous Listening Leader.

There is no downside and you can pave the way for the success of your company. You will motivate your people and even in the most difficult restructuring process or integration after a merger, listening to stakeholders can only make you stronger. With the backing of stakeholders even the most challenging crisis can be managed. The average employee of your company will engage and become a true ambassador. Not a brainwashed member of a cult preaching your gospel, but a mature member of the community, able to convey the magic of what makes your company special and precious to its customers.

The secret is revealed at the end: the power is on your side

What we have been discussing here has an impact on the distribution of power within companies and within society.

There is a dimension here that could appeal to those who want to understand where communicative leadership relocated that power, the ability to shape things.

Companies detain power: the power to create wealth, the power of money to invest and to pay for employment and tax payments.

Companies themselves, however, depend on the power of the good employee to quit, of the customer to buy and recommend or to boycott a product, the power of the investor who buys or sells our share, the power of society who grants us the license to operate or withdraws it.

Communicative leadership can help to balance these powers to the mutual benefit of all stakeholders. The constant listening and communication process with the stakeholders becomes the real power itself, becoming the device to trade off their interests.

If trust is the main commodity of today and tomorrow, power will be detained by those who hoard and accumulate that commodity. Power will be detained by those who have learnt to gain credibility through meaningful information. Those who have learnt to listen intensely and are able to translate this input into the strategy of the company. Power will be in the hands of those who gain the trust of their stakeholders by enabling them, leveraging their strengths and those who redistribute their power to multiply it through the stakeholders.

Power is in the hands of the Listening Leader, that's the little secret revealed on the last pages of this book.

It's the honest, environmentally sound, biological power of the five senses and it's sixth sibling, common sense.

How do you recognise the Listening Leader?

In the end, there are two ways to recognise a Listening Leader taking the initiative to change:

1. **Ability:** The Listening Leader is able to listen and to implement many or all of the suggestions found in this book. They have been tested; I've practised most of them myself and made enough mistakes to help others learn from them with this book.

2. **Awareness:** The second mark that distinguishes the Listening Leader is the awareness that communicative leadership is an opportunity to make business a better place and its role in society more accepted.

There is a difference between being tolerated and owning a license to operate, granted by customers, employees, investors and society at large. It makes it easier for politicians and regulators to leave enough entrepreneurial freedom to corporate citizens who have the support of voters.

In a compelling article in the *Harvard Business Review* the authors write: 'New research suggests that customers and prospective employees aren't the only ones who might be influenced by social responsibility.'[1] Social responsibility addresses society at large as a stakeholder. This means also being accepted by those who can change the rules of the game. Those who work in banking will know what I mean: the room for entrepreneurial manoeuvring has strongly diminished and even central bankers and regulators admit that the old levels of profitability of banks aren't possible any longer after regulatory intervention. This is in spite of the crucial role of banks for our economic system.

Make sure you don't find yourself in that corner. It depends on you and your courage and ability to listen. It depends on your awareness that you can make the difference for yourself, for your team, for your company.

It's about the gift King Solomon asked the Lord in the Book of Kings, quoted at the beginning of this book: an understanding heart, which, as we know from that story, wouldn't only bring you judgement. Richness and long life would follow suit.

Good luck.

Chapter

7

Afterword: Away with corporate communicators?

- Does a company made of Listening Leaders still need a corporate communications department?
- The crossway for communicators: blue ocean or red ocean?
- What is needed to become a communicator of the blue ocean.
- A new value proposition for communicators: contribute to profitable growth.

If you are neither in corporate communications nor a CEO you can skip this chapter altogether.

If you want to save yourself a week in sunny Orvieto in Umbria where in my summer camp I teach communicative leadership, you may find this chapter an interesting alternative to wasting your time learning, accompanied by great food, good company and lots of interaction in one of the most beautiful and culture-rich landscapes of my home country.

In 2006, with my colleague and friend Claudia Reichmuth, we wrote a piece with the title 'Away with communicators!' It was the first time we tried to pin down what we had practised at Allianz.[1] The response (or lack of response) it received – with very few exceptions – told us that we were either totally off track or maybe slightly too aggressive in claiming the end of corporate communications.

Today, I'm convinced we simply were too early. The corporate world hadn't had the time to digest and reflect upon the havoc created by Enron and the mortgage crisis in the United States. The surge of customer-related KPIs like NPS was not yet linked to the overall transformation of a company. We were still munching solely on the remnants of the decades of shareholder value.

What prompted Allianz to engage in the journey of communicative leadership was a board meeting at the turn of the century.

Bad marks on succession planning

The item on the agenda of the executive board was the discussion of succession planning for the most important positions in our company. When it came to my position, the head of group communications, my embarrassment grew and I truly hoped it didn't transpire. The gentlemen around the table said nice words about me, how I was the right man in the job and all sorts of nice stuff. I smelled something coming up. I was right. The CEO drily said that my leadership team around the globe was not up to the new challenges and that it would be hard to find a successor should I fall in love with a Brazilian salsa dancer and move to Rio. I knew what was behind this message. I wasn't up to the new challenges either, and this was the face-saving way the top people of Allianz had just told me.

More knowledge of our core businesses was needed, the ability to interact at eye-level with underwriters, claims people, fund managers and all the smart lawyers and brainy actuaries that make up a company running insurance and asset management operations.

If this wasn't a wake-up call, I don't know what would have been. I stammered something like I needed to discuss this with my boss one-on-one and then I would come back to the board with a proposal.

I prepared myself thoroughly for the meeting with my CEO. I discussed the issue with my most senior team members and I was confronted with some hefty messages by them. The C-suite may be right in considering us simple communications experts but our job was to sweep away the dirt they left us dealing with. Almost every communications crisis we had to manage could have been avoided with some basic understanding about communication by line managers and staff at large.

I didn't like the way this was going. It seemed as if they hadn't heard the message about 'us' and wanted to reply with a message about 'them'. It's not our fault, they said, it's the managers' inability to handle most situations with some common sense. What mattered were legal terms and algorithms and not the story behind it, the people, the customers.

Fortunately, our chief legal counsel had his office in the same building as mine, actually exactly the room below me, one floor down. I went to see him and asked for his advice.

If you're a communications person, you might fathom our conversation. You expect our top lawyer to stress that our role is to teach the press about the legal intricacies of our contracts, our claim settlement practise and our underwriting.

Far away from the truth. This man is the perfect example of what a good chief legal counsel is. Of course he knows almost everything he needs to know about the liability law in most countries and about how to fight in courts. But he is also a very cultivated father and a manager gifted with loads of common sense.

What he told me was surprising: 'Yes,' he said, 'we all need to become better communicators.' God bless him! That was what we needed to do. Transform communicators into managers and managers into communicators.

I then went to see the global head of human resources. I asked what he might do to help us with training our management in the basics of effective communications. He honestly answered that he hadn't given a thought to this challenge, but he was about to create a corporate university and that we might well work together to make this a compulsory part of top management training. That was the breakthrough.

We prepared a presentation for our CEO that lay the groundwork for communicative leadership at Allianz. We used a very simple picture to illustrate the endeavour.

At our next meeting, I was bold enough to propose a deal to the company: we would set up a programme called the Certified Communicator. This would be a mix of an assessment and a development measure. All communicators who wanted to apply for a more senior job than the one they held would have to undergo this programme and be endowed with the blue passport. Only this passport would entitle them to get a better job. Nobody was forced to take it, but without it, career advancement would be impossible. At this programme they would be taught all the basics of our core

▶

businesses, based on the annual report, on interaction with the C-suite in strategic workshops, on an assessment with role-plays and a comprehensive knowledge test.

I saw my boss smiling. That was what he wanted. I'm not sure whether he wanted the second part.

What I had presented was only the communicator's part of the deal, however. This effort would only really help the company succeed if the management would respond to my commitment with equal currency. We would do our best to improve the business knowledge and quality of the communicators. In turn, the management of the company had to learn how to communicate effectively. This would allow us to pre-empt crises at an early stage but also to improve our leadership (as shown in Figure 7.1, illustrating the yin yang of communicative leadership).

He listened to me and with the matter-of-fact-attitude of the real leader he simply said, 'Yes, go for it.'

That's how we started to train hundreds and hundreds of managers in effective communication and how we assessed dozens and dozens of communications people who won their blue passport. Among them, my successor. To prove the point at the beginning, that I would be able to provide the company with a solid succession plan. And I didn't leave for a Brazilian salsa dancer, by the way, but to start a new professional career.

Figure 7.1 The yin yang of communicative leadership

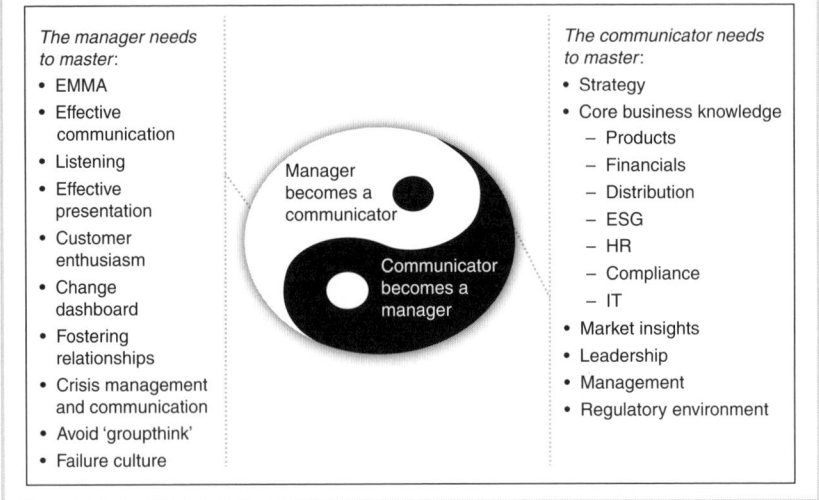

The manager needs to master:
- EMMA
- Effective communication
- Listening
- Effective presentation
- Customer enthusiasm
- Change dashboard
- Fostering relationships
- Crisis management and communication
- Avoid 'groupthink'
- Failure culture

Manager becomes a communicator

Communicator becomes a manager

The communicator needs to master:
- Strategy
- Core business knowledge
  - Products
  - Financials
  - Distribution
  - ESG
  - HR
  - Compliance
  - IT
- Market insights
- Leadership
- Management
- Regulatory environment

This book is mostly about the things I learnt in management development and how to train managers to become Listening Leaders.

This chapter, in turn, is about what is necessary for corporate communications people to become accepted partners for the business.

The old paradigm of corporate communications is that of a mumbling number-cruncher in a pinstripe suit and a multi-million-dollar-salary speaking in Cobol and Java (I said it's the *old* paradigm!) and pushing the punch-card under the door to the PR-person's office, where a cosmopolitan, extroverted former journalist would translate the punch-card into *employese, shareholderese, customerese* and *societese*, the languages of four distinct stakeholder groups.

With the revolution of social media and the empowerment of the individual, as well as with the surge of the average citizen as the most trustworthy source in society and the average employee as the most credible source in a corporation a new paradigm is necessary.

That of communicative leadership, where the corporate communications people help set up a stakeholder governance and organise the exercise of listening to the stakeholders and making sure that this input is discussed within the company and finally used to adapt the strategy. A communications function that doesn't only react well to crises or manages the reputation of the company, but a function that truly contributes to profitable growth.

We discussed this approach in a workshop with some peers from globally operating corporations with the support of the Arthur Page Society as well as challenging it with world-class communications scholars like Toni Muzi Falconi, then New York University who asked me to provide the Allianz case for a book that finally appeared in 2014, with the contribution of the *doyen* of communication research, Jim Grunig of Maryland.[2]

Does good corporate communications correlate with profitable growth?

Yes it does. In the project done with Bain and Media Tenor and briefly mentioned in Chapter 2 we looked at best and worst practices in our company.

We picked five subsidiaries that were so-called loyalty leaders. According to the terminology of Bain, the company that discovered the impact of the Net Promoter Score, loyalty leaders are companies with the strongest NPS in their market. In other words, those companies that lead profitable growth in their markets by the highest enthusiasm of their customers, or the top rate of recommendations from one customer to another. Then we picked four loyalty laggards. These are the companies that constantly shrink in their markets, losing customers.

Then we looked at two key performance indicators: the engagement of their employees according to the global Engagement Survey as well as their media awareness and the tonality of the media reporting as monitored by our media analysis institute.

The result was absolutely adamant: the loyalty leaders had both outstanding track-records in media communications and internal communications, the two crown disciplines of corporate communications (see Figure 7.2).

The scientists among you will ask two questions, I presume: Understood that there is a strong correlation. By the way, was it

Figure 7.2 Leadership culture survey and employment engagement index indicate that employee communication is also relevant to NPS

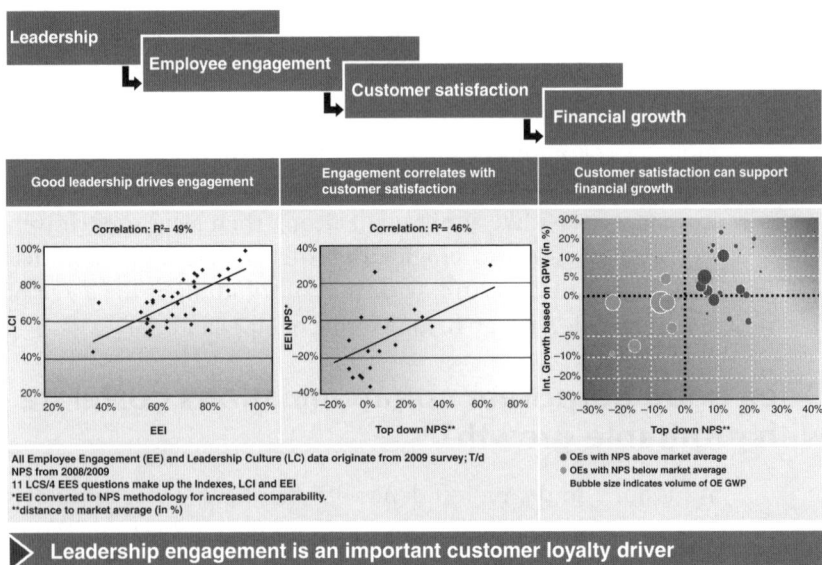

Source: adapted from Allianz SE

higher than R3? Yes it was. The second question will be: Accepted that there is a strong correlation, where's the causality? Is the company growing because of good corporate communications or does a company growing profitably have a CEO who understands the importance of media and internal communications and practises it to a high standard?

Actually for the purpose of this book and the practice behind: I couldn't care less about the answer. Because what works is the yin yang, both efforts paying into one account. Good leadership and good corporate communications both drive profitable growth.

On agenda-setting media...

Every corporation has to be aware of the importance of the so-called agenda-setting media. They can kill your reputation in a second. It's those quality media like the *Financial Times*, *The Economist* or the BBC in the United Kingdom, but also the major dailies, including the tabloids. In Germany it would be the public TV, *Der Spiegel* and dailies like the *Frankfurter Allgemeine Zeitung*, *Süddeutsche Zeitung* and the tabloid *BILD*. And so on for CNN, *The Wall Street Journal*, the *New York Times* and *Washington Post* in the United States, *Le Monde*, *Le Figaro*, Public TV in France and you can fill in the boxes for all major countries.

These media set the agenda. Every corporation has to be fully aware that it needs to be sure to have a constant presence in those media, always above the media awareness threshold.

Why, actually? Isn't it smarter to keep a very low profile in the media, especially these media, known for good investigative journalism and their independence? It may seem so, until you're faced with a crisis. A corporate crisis will always trigger the interest of the agenda-setting media, and normally a bad situation turns into a crisis *because* of the reports on that difficult situation by these media.

The only way to survive a corporate crisis covered by agenda-setting media is to constantly be present in these media by your own initiative. Interesting interviews, op-ed pieces, research of public interest by your company, comments and press releases on market relevant issues: make sure that the amount of regular reporting breaks the sound barrier of public awareness. You better track this media presence day by day, month by month through one of the few media analysis companies who can explain to you what the media awareness threshold *is* in every market. It's your duty as a PR professional, to make sure that you generate constant coverage. Should the inevitable moment of a corporate crisis come, this amount of reporting will help you to buffer the effect of a crisis. People will read about the crisis but they will also associate your brand with all the good output you had generated before and hopefully continue to generate, giving you some credit for it, credit you can benefit from in a crisis.

There's an obvious second reason that should encourage you as a PR professional to entertain frequent interactions with reporters from agenda-setting media: you get to know the reporters on your beat. Through them you will be able to understand what readers (or viewers) expect from your products and your company at large.

Agenda-setting media reach all stakeholders of a company. Their impact on purchasing behaviours of customers is smaller than their impact on the overall reputation of the company, at the beginning. It takes a prolonged period of negative reporting not counterbalanced by any reaction to slowly change consumer patterns until they reach a tipping point from which it is then difficult – or impossible – to recover.

Research on the mutual influence of traditional and social media hasn't really shed light on when power shifts from the one to the other and under which conditions. From practice we know that traditional agenda-setting media now use social media themselves, both to market their outlets and news and to gather information from social media sources. In other words, both matter and both increasingly influence each other, sometimes in a surprisingly simplistic way: a European newspaper decides on its printed front page edition based on the page views of their online edition at deadline. Which brings about the Waterloo of quality journalism. But it is what it is and a corporate communications professional needs to adapt to the chameleon-like mutations of journalism in these years.

The interaction of social media and agenda-setting outlets

Increasingly, blogs and social media platforms are becoming sources equal to a CEO or another C-suite member for agenda-setting media. A company statement is mirrored by a statement of a customer in the blogosphere or a disgruntled employee on the many new platforms where people can anonymously voice their thoughts and information on employers.

The average citizens are empowered by social media and gain a public voice as individuals. Plus, they become the source for agenda-setting media – with more weight than the C-suite or the PR people.

I was sitting at a fireplace in the middle of nowhere in the Masai Mara, in Kenya. I was a guest of my friend Riccardo Orizio, an old-hand of investigative journalism, writer of books on dictators and lost white tribes on our planet, a friend of the late Richard Kapuzcinski, whom he worked with to set up three marvellous lodges in Kenya. We were speaking of how the journalistic profession had changed and I asked him whether political reporting was somehow affected by online reporting.

He told me the story of 19-year-old Thomas Van Linge, an Amsterdam student. The war correspondents covering Syria, Iraq or Libya all know him very well. He is a regular source to CNN, *The New York Times* and *Der Spiegel*, even though he has never set foot in those crisis areas. Why on earth should these agenda-setting media rely on him as a source and for what? Thomas van Linge makes 'some of the world's best maps of chaotic war zones from the desk of his childhood bedroom in Amsterdam'.[3] 'He Skypes with fighters on the front, corresponds with activists and charities and even gets messages from other cartographers. In all, he claims to use over 1,100 sources for his Syrian maps.' In easy-to-understand colours you can regularly track the areas controlled by ISIS or the government forces in Syria. You can follow him on his Twitter account @ arabthomness.

An average citizen equipped with a computer and a Twitter account has become an important source for the general press.

On customer-relevant media

Next to agenda-setting media it is crucial to become aware of the media which drive customer recommendations. These media only very rarely are agenda-setting media, and if they are, it's normally the tabloids who have one foot in each camp, the one shaping a company's reputation and the other adding or subtracting customers.

Most of the customers are influenced by social media and more specialised media outlets. How to reach out to customers is the almost precise science of big data and that's what good market management or marketing people do. Corporate communications people who don't work hand in hand with their marketing colleagues are destroying value for the company. Media communicators need to perfectly know which media drive consumer behaviour, whether it's social or traditional media, specialist magazines or blogs or YouTube channels.

This analysis comes first. Then comes the constant monitoring and interacting with these media. Corporate communicators working in companies using customer KPIs like NPS have to have a clear map of the media that drive the reputational agenda of the general public and of those who drive customer behaviour and they have to serve both.

With social media we step into the new world, altogether. While journalists are used to working with corporate communications and relate to common ethical and professional standards, this is not true with social media, the media of the empowered average citizen. They can only be tackled with the full support of the average citizens within your organisation, all the employees. More on this in the next section on the blue ocean of communications.

The first conclusion of our project was finding a sound correlation between customer recommendations and media work. It is necessary, therefore, to change the media work. It is necessary to separately consider, treat and interact with agenda-setting media (that's good practice in most companies, anyway), customer-relevant media (this needs to be better aligned with purchasing patterns, marketing and customer KPIs than it has been previously) and social media (that's new, altogether, because it involves the commitment and action of all leaders and, ultimately, all employees).

So far, we are still more or less in the old world, in the red ocean of communications. Red because of the blood of harsh competition, of sharks eating barracudas and barracudas eating maccarels and so forth. Its the traditional world of corporate communications with its old core discipline media relations, even though applied to the new media, as well, more or less with the same professional toolkit.

The real challenge starts with transforming the whole organisation, becoming the sounding board and enabling partner of the Listening Leaders within the organisation and with and through them with the whole staff of the company.

The blue ocean of communicative leadership

Next to the red ocean of PR there is a new, largely undiscovered blue sea for communications professionals, still uncoloured by the blood of competition, because there is almost none. Very few companies have started to practise communicative leadership and very few communications professionals are equipped with the proper tools for this blue ocean, yet.

While communicative leadership aims to transform a company it also needs a new breed of corporate communicators to succeed.

Today's and tomorrow's challenge is to wire all the internal and external connections of a company into a neuronal network that constantly communicates. The role of the communicators is like the role of neurotransmitters in our brains, they have to connect the dots. Well beyond the old ivory tower of corporate communications, confined to a dialogue with top management only acting more or less as their loudspeakers or, in the better cases, as their translators.

Corporate communicators in the new world of the blue ocean basically have four roles:

1. **Monitor internal and external audience:** Map the stakeholders, monitor and analyse and create a stakeholder governance. This will mean new job opportunities for *mathematicians, IT specialists and analysts* in corporate communications departments.

2. **Enable management:** Join hips and efforts with all the other corporate functions, from HR, marketing, IT, sales, operations, investor and governmental relations, compliance to ESG office and CSR in order to ensure that internal stakeholders are enabled and empowered to practise meaningful information and communication. Communicators will therefore have to learn to teach and educate or seek help from *professional educators* joining their ranks in corporate communications.

3. **Ensure good listening:** Be the stewards of EMMA, of state-of-the-art corporate listening throughout the organisation, on behalf and with the full support of the C-suite. This means strong empathy will be the crucial recruitment factor for new staff: *psychologists* can enrich corporate communications teams.

4. **Drive change:** Make sure that the organisation hears what was said and constantly challenges and adapts its strategy accordingly. This calls for *strategy specialists, change management experts, people with a management consultancy background and MBAs* to join corporate communications.

To achieve this, a much stronger cooperation is needed between corporate communications and the other company functions.

In order to successfully manage the transition to a new balance in stakeholder governance and finally to communicative leadership, language trainings are needed. The corporate communicators need to learn the language of business, of operations, sales, HR, IT, product development and delivery, compliance and so on. And these corporate functions need to learn the language of listening, EMMA.

This is exactly why we have invested so much time at Allianz to invest in corporate education and setting up the Allianz Communication Academy. It offers courses from media-training for the new world of blue ocean to 'Becoming an Accepted Adviser' or 'Being a Trusted Sparring Partner to the C-suite' to 'Voice and Body Language'. The good thing about this programme is: These courses are open for participants from any other company, provided the participant speaks English and pays for it.[4] That's where listening is learnt and taught. The better the listening quality of corporate communications is, the more likely it is that they teach managers and staff.

That's why *recruitment* of communications professionals will change. From the traditional reserve of journalists, politicians and PR people from not-for-profit organisations, corporate communications departments will need to recruit more behavioural psychologists, educators and trainers, marketing people, big data analysts and mathematicians as well as more people with a law or business education, expertise in strategy and business development.

Furthermore the *exchange between the corporate functions has to be strongly increased*. Communicators have to spend time working with the other corporate functions, learning their processes and teaching them listening. Communication departments need to host colleagues from other departments to see how the different functions shape the reputation of the organisation.

Never forget that reputation is nothing more (or less) than sustainable behaviour. The purpose of these staff exchanges is therefore to understand how the behaviours of the company impact the stakeholders and whether it transforms them into detractors or promoters of the company.

Some comfort from academia

Academia is often, as it happens, in the lead. Even though it is seldom perceived as such by practitioners. What listening means from a strategic point of view to communicators was addressed by Maria Borner, University of Leipzig, in her master thesis on corporate listening (2015).[5] She criticises that in practice corporate communication is often misunderstood as simply one-way messaging. She defines corporate listening as a strategic mode of communication, in which articulated impulses from stakeholders are perceived, interpreted and evaluated in order to support the company's decision-making process, or, in other words, its strategy. The analytical counterpart is corporate messaging, conveying content. It is a strategic decision whether the communication function focuses on corporate messaging or on corporate listening. She understands corporate listening as a major communication mode, expressed in the structures, strategies, processes and measures of corporate communications and beyond, on all levels of the corporation. In this way listening can create value through enabling operations, adjusting strategy, creating intangibles and

ensuring flexibility. It's worthwhile reading if you look for an academically sound perspective on this issue.

Learning, learning, learning

Communicators furthermore have to undergo learning themselves: on the new media work, on leadership, on motivation, talent development and most other HR practices, on business
matters and on strategy.

They are the first that have to undergo the training outlined in
Chapter 3 on 'Enabling': strategy, customer focus, listening, crisis
management and crisis communications, effective communications, effective presentation and integrated reporting.

(Mystery) shopping

Communications professionals of the blue ocean have to have their
ear to the ground of the prairie, able to hear the bisons coming.
They should use the products of their own employer, unless you
sell steam engines. If this is the case, talk to those who buy your
engines. Experience your products and services as much as you can.
Every year every communications professional should spend a
week in the shoes of the company's customer.

The result for the customer

We have seen the importance of having a strong KPI per stakeholder. We have also seen that a more comprehensive yearly reporting process to the public should be provided, next to the standard
annual report with the financial results. There is one stakeholder
that we mostly care for, though, the customer. Why? Because an
enthusiastic customer is at the beginning of the virtuous circle. An
enthusiastic customer will recommend your company and this will
drive profitable growth. That's exactly what investors are interested
in. Only committed, enabled, empowered and therefore motivated
employees can drive the customer experience to a 10. This will create employment, increase payments to the tax man and provide a
reason for being of this good corporate citizen to society at large.

What's the conclusion? Do you remember the example in Chapter 1 of an airline that would publish its safety compared to that

of the competitors, benchmark punctuality, service, prices and offers? Wouldn't you be surprised to read in plain talk what still doesn't work in customer delivery, benchmarked to competitors. Wouldn't this increase the credibility of this company?

Let's then imagine a yearly 'Result for the Customer' report that tells customers (and all other parties interested), how your company performed in customer delivery, product quality and servicing of the customers. Written in plain language, addressing flaws as well as strengths of the company. Telling single customer stories, good and bad experiences that are symptomatic for that year's performance in respect to the customer. In case of the flaws, the customer would understand where the problem lay and how the company intends to fix it. Wouldn't that create trust? Especially if based on objective data and KPIs. Compared to competitors. Should you not want to name them (out of respect, out of fear for their bad reactions or for whatever other reason), you could simply give them letters from A–X, naming your own company only and showing where it stands in the market.

Believe me, this will invite customers and media to ask your competitors why *they* haven't published these data and how *they* are treating their customers. You would gain a true advantage and set and shape the agenda. Every year you could show your improvements on the way to become the most successful company in the industry. Don't be afraid of the first year or bad results. Honesty and transparency will pay off and this transparency will be there internally, too. All employees would know where to focus in order to improve their customer focus substantially. The first company to have published such a result for The Customer already exists, it's Allianz Deutschland, now for the third year in a row. Be the second one. Or the first to do this, globally. Get ahead of your competitors. Have the endurance and courage to make it a long-term exercise; this only pays off if done consistently over the years, good and bad ones.

Media, the bad guys. Really?

I hear the moaning: media won't follow us on this journey. They don't care about our products and customer feedback unless it's negative. Far from me to defend a whole category, especially since I practised journalism myself and still am a member of the professional journalists association in Italy. But try to do the EMMA exercise with people working for media outlets who have seen the birth of online media and a totally new competitive landscape. This is the biggest revolution in the sector after the widespread use of TV.

If the information is relevant and meaningful, you will find your audience in the media, traditional ones, agenda-setting outlets, blogs and social media. Do as all managers do: map your stakeholders, find out their EMMA and see where their needs converge with your offer. Or create an offer. Stay close to the media and follow their own journey to reinvent themselves and adapt to the change driven by internet.

Constructive news

So, are journalists, tabloids, media manipulative? No, fortunately not, the majority isn't. And how some media reacted to their loss of trust and credibility in the last decade teaches us a useful lesson for business information: don't be negative at all costs. Whenever you describe a negative phenomenon, draw a lesson, show where people dealt constructively with a negative situation. Ulrik Haagerup calls it 'constructive news'. 'Good reporting is seeing the world with both eyes. Not missing the important stories about ebola in West Africa, hunger, bombings in Gaza and Ukraine and millions on the run from terror in Syria. But also seeing stories which can inspire and engage because it shows the opposite; things that work, people doing something extraordinary to solve important problems. The big picture.'[6]

What can we learn from this for business information? That while you should never brush the difficult issues under the carpet, when you do, you can also show how these difficulties are being dealt with constructively elsewhere. We cannot only learn from other experiences, a solution somewhere else can 'inspire and engage' where we are right now.

Why should you do it? Because it's right and fair? Yes, of course. But also because it's successful. Media adopting the constructive news concept of Ulrik fare better in terms of reach and audience than others, starting with the success of Danish TV news, the outlet Ulrik Haagerup is the head of.

Who's the real boss?

> How interconnected stakeholders are and where reputation – good or bad – plants its seeds, is not always a question of media. Communicators should be aware of the impact small behaviours of the organisation can have on big business opportunities. Sometimes lost, because we didn't thoroughly do our homework.

Martin worked for an electro-engineering company, selling almost everything from power plants to white goods. As part of his training to become global head of corporate communications, he spent some time selling the power plants of his employer. One day he has a very important appointment: he is meeting the CEO of a large utility company considering buying one of Martin's company's power plants. Martin is perfectly prepared for the meeting, has learnt everything necessary on the main product features, on safety of the product, on technological edge. He is not an engineer, but his potential customer isn't either. What happens is beyond his imagination. He starts to illustrate the product features and the state-of-the-art technology. Suddenly the CEO uses Martin's pause for breath to ask a simple question: 'How good is your customer service in case of a crisis?' Martin is well prepared and recites the procedures from the customer crisis manual. He sees a very sceptical look in the eyes of the top manager and potential customer. Time to let him translate body language into speech. Which the CEO does: 'Look, I just can't recommend buying your power plants for my company. My wife won't allow me to.'

Martin is flabbergasted. His wife? He swears mutely, reproaching himself for not having done his homework. It's crystal clear that the CEO's wife must be an engineer with the company or a scientist or somebody with strong arguments. That was actually true, but not in the domain Martin suspected. The CEO's wife was a traditional lady managing the household of the family. The CEO explained: 'We bought a washing machine from your company. It broke after one week and your customer service is lousy. We talked to them several times, they tried to put the blame on us and how we were allegedly not able to use the washing machine properly, they read us the

▶

instructions of the machine over the phone as if we couldn't read them ourselves. They lectured us. Nobody has shown up yet to fix the damned thing. Do you want me to buy a power plant from you? How can you guarantee that when there is an accident you don't treat us like you treat my family at home? It's the same company, isn't it?' Average citizens: the guy from the customer service and a housewife had more to say in a multi-million deal than the CEO and the company representative.

Sitting next to the driver seat – but only with a driving licence

It is absolutely unthinkable for a company to grow through communicative leadership without the head of corporate communications sitting at the table of decision making, the executive board or executive committee. She doesn't need to be a member of this body. Actually, I advocate that this would be wrong, allowing all the others to continue business as usual and put the blame of bad communications on the professional board fellow: EVERY leader has to become a communicator. The corporate communicator has to be a facilitator and manage the structured dialogue with stakeholders through a well thought out stakeholder governance.

The steward of stakeholder dialogue therefore has to sit close to the driver seat. If this is not the case, yet, discuss it with the CEO. If your participation at the executive meetings and the board is rejected, make up your mind: stay in the red ocean of the old world and sell your services with the good old toolbox of corporate communications: crisis communication, media relations, internal communications, social media relations. Full stop. Forget blue oceans, your increase in market value by helping to deliver profitable growth through your function and all the nice stuff you've read so far. Just accept being a humble translator of the announcements of the company.

The other choice is: quit. My strong belief is, companies who don't read the writing on the wall of empowered citizens and their trustworthiness as promoters of profitable growth, are doomed, sooner or later. They will not be able to keep and renew their license to operate. By quitting, you might be the first rat (sorry for this) to leave the sinking ship.

Buy yourself *Ultimate Question 2.0* and look up the companies who work with NPS and who got the core message of customer enthusiasm. You'll find a list of excellent employers who would probably jump at the chance of a competent communicator of the blue ocean: Allianz, Apple, Lego, Philips, Progressive and many others. Leave the stubborn employers who don't get the message of good profits behind. Join the winners.

Participation of the chief communications officer in the top governance body's meeting is the litmus test of communicative leadership.

Be careful, though: if you as a communication professional are not up to the challenge, being next to the driver won't help you, it may damage you. The board or executive committee is not the omniscient body. They have to take decisions. But the grounds on which they make these decisions should be owned by the communication professional at the table: the communicator should know better than the C-suite how the average citizen and all the stakeholders perceive the company.

She should be on top of the financials of the company, know the product factory from inside and have experienced the purchase and sale of the company products.

She should then have all the intelligence available to support decision making.

Just sitting at the table, taking notes and smiling politely will make your boss consider a Siberian re-education camp for you. The deal is: the Chief Communication Officer has to contribute to decision making by delivering the voice of the stakeholders and thereby is granted to be a part of modern King Arthur's Camelot, the boardroom.

As we concluded in the piece Claudia and I wrote in 2006, this means a new self-consciousness by the professional communicators, who are not immune from some common top management diseases like vanity. Many like to be the shrewd Machiavelli guiding the helpless number crunchers through the wicked mazes of the media and take over the dialogue with the employees through internal communications.

It's the same conclusion the Arthur Page Society (APS) came to. The APS is an interest group of chief communication officers and researchers, which I'm a member of. The conclusion of their study 'A Building Belief' in 2012 was that the king discipline of the new chief communication officer would be what they called 'Advocacy at Scale': 'Turning changed behavior into active advocacy [of the stakeholders] on behalf of the now-shared agenda.'[7]

Communicators in the blue ocean of communicative leadership enable all managers and finally all employees to entertain the dialogue with stakeholders. They don't take themselves seriously, they take communication seriously.

What did you think of this book?

We're really keen to hear from you about this book, so that we can make our publishing even better.

Please log on to the following website and leave us your feedback.

It will only take a few minutes and your thoughts are invaluable to us.

www.pearsoned.co.uk/bookfeedback

Notes

Introduction

1. 'Trust Meltdown VII: The Financial Industry Needs a Fundamental Restart', edited by Racheline Maltese and Matthias Vollbracht with contributions from Milind Lele, Brian Pallas and Roland Schatz, Innovatio, 2016.

2. www.edelman.com/insights/intellectual-property/2016-edelman-trust-barometer/global-results/

3. *The Ultimate Question: Driving Good Profits and True Growth*, Fred Reichheld, Harvard Business School Press, Boston, Massachusetts, 2006.

4. Deloitte Millennial Survey (2016). Winning over the next generation of leaders.

Chapter 1   Information

1. www.economist.com/styleguide/introduction

2. www.americanpressinstitute.org/journalism-essentials/makes-good-story/

3. www.bullshitbingo.net/cards/bullshit/

4. www.youtube.com/watch?v=yR0lWICH3rY

5. *The Ultimate Question: Driving Good Profits and True Growth*, Fred Reichheld, Harvard Business School Press, Boston, Massachusetts, 2006, p.140.

6. *Enduring Success: What We Can Learn from the History of Outstanding Corporations*, Christian Stadler, Stanford Business Books, 2011, Stanford, California, p.139.

7. *One Report: Integrated Reporting for a Sustainable Strategy*, Robert G. Eccles and Michael P. Krusz, John Wiley & Sons, Inc., 2010, Hoboken, New Jersey.

8. PricewaterhouseCoopers (2007) Corporate reporting – a time for reflection: A survey of the Fortune Global 500 companies' narrative reporting.

9. Statistics for the US come from the following source: SBA Office of Advocacy (2016), United States Small Business Profile. Global statistics come from the following source: Kelley, D., Singer, S. and Herrington, M. (2016) Global Entrepreneurship Monitor 2015/16 Global Report.

10. *The Hidden Persuaders*, Vance Packard, Pocket Books, Inc., New York, 1957.

11. Barton, C., Koslow, L. and Beauchamp, C. (2014). How millennials are changing the face of marketing forever. BCG Perspectives. Retrieved from www.bcgperspectives.com/content/articles/marketing_center_consumer_customer_insight_how_millennials_changing_marketing_forever/?chapter=3#chapter3

Chapter 2   Communication

1. *Together – The Rituals, Pleasures and Politics of Co-operation*, Richard Sennett, Penguin Books Ltd, London, 2012, pp. 18–20.

2. Peter Záboji, *Change! Gestalten Sie heute Ihr Unternehmen von morgen*, Verlag Moderne Industrie, 2001, p. 213.

3. *Time to Think*, Nancy Kline, Ward Lock Cassell Illustrated, Octopus Publishing Group, London, 1999, ed. 2013, p. 59.

4. Richard Sennett, ibidem, p. 24.

5. *The Financial Times Guide to Business Coaching*, Anne Scoular, Pearson Education Limited, Harlow, 2011, p. 76.

6. Nancy Kline, ibidem, p. 53.

7. Frederickson, Barbara L. (2013) Updated thinking on positivity ratios, *American Psychologist*, 15 July. Advance online publication; doi: 10.1037/a0033584

8. *NLP at Work, Neuro Linguistic Programming, The Essence of Excellence*, Sue Knight, Nicholas Brealey Publishing, London, Boston, Third Edition, 2009.

9. *Love 'Em or Lose 'Em – Getting Good People To Stay. 26 Engagement Strategies for Busy Managers*, Beverly Kaye and Sharon Jordan-Evans, Berrett-Koehler Publishers, 2014.

10. *The Ultimate Question: Driving Good Profits and True Growth*, Fred Reichheld, Harvard Business School Press, Boston, Massachusetts, 2006.

11. Deloitte Millennial Survey (2014). Big demands and high expectations.

Chapter 3   Enabling

1. *Drive: The Surprising Truth About What Motivates Us*, Daniel H. Pink (2009), Canongate Books Ltd, Edinburgh, UK.

2. *The 5 Languages of Appreciation in the Workplace – Empowering Organizations by Encouraging People*, Gary Chapman and Paul White, Northfield Publishing, 2011–2012, Chicago, US.

3. *Love 'Em or Lose 'Em – Getting Good People to Stay. 26 Engagement Strategies for Busy Managers*, Beverly Kaye and Sharon Jordan-Evans, Berrett-Koehler Publishers, Inc., San Francisco, 2008.

4. *State of the American Manager – Analytics and Advice for Leaders*, Gallup, 2015, p.18.

5. *The Wisdom of Teams – Creating the High-performance Organization*, Jon R. Katzenbach, Douglas K. Smith, Harvard Business Press and McGraw-Hill Publishing Company, Maidenhead, 1993.

6. Read also *How: Why How We Do Anything Means Everything … in business (and in life)*, Dov Seidman, John Wiley & Sons, Hoboken, New Jersey, 2007.

7. Adapted from: Janis, 1972; Baron and Greenberg 1990 and 1996; Zander 1982, as quoted in Furnham, A. (1998), *The Psychology of Behaviour in Organisations*, Psychology Press: London, pp. 500–503.

8. http://insights.ccl.org/articles/leading-effectively-articles/the-70-20-10-rule/

9. *Love 'Em or Lose 'Em – Getting Good People to Stay. 26 Engagement Strategies for Busy Managers*, Beverly Kaye and Sharon Jordan-Evans, Berrett-Koehler Publishers, Inc., San Francisco, 2008.

10. *The AMA Handbook of Leadership*, Marshall Goldsmith, John Baldoni, Sarah McArthur, American Management Association, 2010, US.

11. *Dialogische Führung*, Karl-Martin Dietz, Thomas Kracht, Campus Verlag, Frankfurt/New York, 2007.

12. *The Theory of Moral Sentiments*, Adam Smith, Liberty Fund Press, Indianapolis, 1982, p. 21.

13. *Empathy*, Roman Krznaric, Rider, an imprint of Ebury Publishing, Random House Group, 2015.

14. Stahl, G. K. et al. (2012). Six principles of effective global talent management, *MIT Sloan Management Review*, 53(2), 25–32.

15. Rynes, S. L., Brown, K. G. and Colbert, A. E. (2002). Seven common misconceptions about human resource practices: research findings versus and practitioner beliefs, *Academy of Management Executive*, 16(3), 92–103.

16. Sanders, K., Van Riemsdijk, M. and Groen, B. (2008). The gap between research and practice: a replication study on the HR professionals, *International Journal of Human Resource Management*, 19(10), 1976–88.

Chapter 4   Empowerment

1. *Business Coaching – Financial Times Guides*, Anne Scoular, Pearson Education Limited, Harlow, UK, 2011, p. 7.

2. Ibidem, p. 1.

3. *Coaching for Performance – GROWing human potential and purpose. The principles and practice of coaching and leadership*, Sir John Whitmore, Nicholas Brealey Publishing, London, 2009, p. 55.

4. http://humanresources.about.com/od/glossarym/g/mentoring.htm

5. *Insolvent und Trotzdem Erfolgreich*, Anne Koark, Insolvenzverlag, Bad Nauheim, 2007.

6. *The Big Five for Life: Leadership's Greatest Secret. Was wirklich zählt im Leben*, John Strelecky, German edition, Deutscher Taschenbuch Verlag GmbH & Co. KG, München, 2013.

7. *The Cosmopolitan*, Kwame Anthony Appiah, W.W. Norton, New York, 2006.

8. *Monkey Management – Wie Manager in weniger Zeit mehr erreichen*, Dr Jan Roy Edlund, Monenstein und Vannerdat OHG Münster, 2010.

9. This observation was famously made and then further examined by social psychologist Geert Hofstede in the latter half of the twentieth century. His framework of cultural dimensions is

considered a hallmark of cultural research within many fields including psychology, sociology and anthropology.

10. Harvard IOP Spring 2016 Poll. Harvard Institute of Politics.

Chapter 5 The Listening Leader in action

1. *Pragmatics of Human Communication: A Study of Interactional Patterns, Pathologies and Paradoxes*, Paul Watzlawick, Janet Beavin Bavelas and Don D. Jackson, W. W. Norton & Company, New York, USA, 2011.

2. *Buddha's Brain - the practical neuroscience of happiness, love and wisdom*, Richard Hanson, Ph.D. with Richard Mendius, MD, New Harbinger Publications Inc. Oakland, CA, USA, 2009.

3. Ibidem, pp. 68–69.

4. Ibidem, p. 1.

5. *Working Identity: Unconventional Strategies for Reinventing your Career*, Herminia Ibarra, Harvard Business School Press, Boston, 2003.

Chapter 6 Conclusion

1. *Crime, Punishment and the Halo Effect of Corporate Social Responsibility*, Harrison Hong and Inessa Liskovich, quoted in *Harvard Business Review*, November 2015, page 32.

Chapter 7 Afterword

1. 'Schafft die Kommunikatoren ab!' Emilio Galli Zugaro and Claudia Reichmuth in Palais Biron, *Das Magazin für Vordenker*, Baden Badener Unternehmergespräche, Baden-Baden, Nr. 6/Winter 2008.

2. *Global Stakeholder Relationships Governance: An Infrastructure*, Toni Muzi Falconi, James Grunig, Emilio Galli Zugaro, Joao Duarte, Palgrave Macmillan, New York, 2014.

3. www.spiegel.de/international/world/how-thomas-van-linge-mapped-islamic-state-a-1048665.html

4. 'Communications Academy 2016.' For non-Allianz companies, www.allianz.com

5. Borner, Maria (2015) *Corporate Listening in Corporate Communication. A theoretical foundation of organisational listening as a strategic mode of communication.* University of Leipzig, Leipzig. (unpublished master thesis)

6. *Constructive News,* Ulrik Haagerup, InnoVatio Publishing, Hanoi, New York, Pretoria, Rapperswil, 2014, p. 4.

7. www.awpagesociety.com/news/arthur-w-page-society-unveils-new-model-for-corporate-communications/

Acknowledgments

Communicative leadership, as it is described in this book, is the sum of ideas, experiences, research and practice by many people and I don't pretend to be anything other than the storyteller of this philosophy. It was developed within Allianz, my former employer, and it was enriched by contributions from many people, all of whom I cannot thank here. There are some that need to be mentioned, though.

Henning Schulte-Noelle, CEO of Allianz from 1992 to 2003 mentored me through my growth as a manager. A great listener himself, he struck that important deal that allowed communicative leadership to be born, the yin yang where the communicator learns the business and turns into a manager and where the manager becomes a communicator, or a Listening Leader.

Michael Diekmann, CEO between 2003 and 2015, another superb listener, guided Allianz through quite a rocky period during two global financial crises. It's in times of crises when you see of what fabric a leader is made: he never relented on the importance of HR and corporate communications when the going got rough. For him, a promise is a promise.

It was an honour to serve Allianz for more than two decades.

The present CEO, Oliver Bäte, I've known for a dozen years and in my last year at Allianz we worked closely together. Before starting his new job he went on an intensive listening tour and now this pays off. I thank him for having allowed me to write this book, contractual obligations I had with Allianz made it necessary for a consent to mention the firm.

Within my team and among my colleagues at Allianz many supported me and, again, there is not enough room to mention all of them. But without Sonia Allinson-Penny, Steven Althaus, Berengere Auguste-Dormheuil, Susanne Bluhm, Silke Bonarius, Renate Braun, Patience Chan, Fabio Dal Boni, Rosa De Simone, Daniel Dirks, Christian Finckh, Flavia Genillard, Joe Gross, Bernd Heinemann, Kristine Helbig, Wolfgang Ischinger, Hugo Kidston, Hermann Knipper, Viktoria Kranz, Christian Kroos, Ulf Lange, Dominique

Legrand, Thomas Loesler, Stefan Lutz, Anne Marchegay, Laura Marsi, Pedro Martins, Luisa Masetto, Lars Mielke, Claudia Mohr-Calliet, Hans-Peter Nehmer, Mani Pillai, Claudia Reichmuth, Stefan Rastorfer, Marita Roloff, Stephanie Schneider, Sabia Schwarzer, Petra Seeger-Kelbe, Dan Tarman, Nick Tewes, Gesa Walter, Nikki Whitfield, John Wallace, Reiner Wolf and Christopher Worthley, communicative leadership wouldn't exist as it is today. Not to forget two chief legal counsels like Bernd Honsel and Peter Hemeling, who understand the mechanics of communications better than many PR professionals and helped me to understand the intricacies of compliance and legal issues.

It's a tragedy that three of the most important contributors to communicative leadership are no longer with us. Ellen Heather, Lothar Landgraf and Antje Weykopf were at the forefront of our efforts and – literally until they passed away – were role models for communicative leadership.

I owe research a lot. Number one to receive this credit is Toni Muzi Falconi, an icon of Italian corporate communications but also a charismatic Professor at IULM and New York University, with whom I had many controversial and highly productive conversations on the subject of this book. In 2013 he asked me to contribute to his book on stakeholder governance and in 2014 it was the first time the concept of communicative leadership became public. Thank you, Toni.

The work with Konstantin Korotov, Zoltan Antal Mokos, Gregor Halff, Urs Müller and Franziska Frank at the ESMT in Berlin has strengthened my belief in communicative leadership and I owe the students of the executive programmes for their input, questions and feedback. Jorg Rocholl, the dean of ESMT, and his predecessor Wulf Plinke deserve a medal for their patience with me.

Mark Hunter from INSEAD was a precious challenger of communicative leadership at a jointly held workshop on corporate compliance and investigative journalism. A true listener.

Andreas Bittl from Ludwig-Maximilians-Universität in Munich, now an Allianz manager, was the first to make me aware of the business impact of trust. That was prescient in 1997.

Discussions with Bob Eccles and Mike Krusz from Harvard on trust and integrated reporting inspired me in manifold ways.

I wouldn't be what I am today without the appearance of Meyler Campbell (MC) in my horizons. The coaching school in London and their business coach programme from which I have graduated in

2015 have impacted the refinement of communicative leadership. Large parts of this book are inspired by what I learned at MC and discussed with my great tutor Ann Orton and my fellow graduates Claudia Danser and Duncan Aldred. Without the nuclear energy of Anne Scoular, the founder of Meyler Campbell, I wouldn't have found the courage to write this book. She also introduced me to my agent and coaching colleague Liz Gooster whom I owe for the perfect match with Pearson, my publisher.

This world would have been out of my reach if not for Nancy Glynn, a former corporate communications executive, now coach and my supervisor. Nancy introduced me to Anne Scoular and Meyler Campbell and thereby ignited the flow of knowledge, coaching practice and relationships that led to this book.

David Waller, a prolific author, former FT journalist and corporate comms colleague at Allianz and FTI and a dear friend inspired me throughout the last 20 years of my professional life and has challenged this book in an intense one-day workshop at my house in Orvieto. With Nancy and Claudia he read a first draft of the book and their remarks have improved this book remarkably. Also part of that spring day in Umbria was Filippo Muzi Falconi, CEO of Methodos S.p.A., the Change Management Company based in Milan that I chair. With him was Viola Pagnoni. They brought their enormous experience in change management to the table under the portico.

Luca Argenton, Marcello Fontana, Giulio Gallana, Sabrina Paladini, Livia Piermattei and Alessio Vaccarezza from Methodos challenged communicative leadership from a change management and leadership practice point of view and how clients could react to a strategic offer on these matters.

Toni Anders, Gabriele Kaminski, John Mengers, Stefan Reckhenrich and my old school-friend Hans Thoenes are superior executive search specialists (what we call headhunters) and were all crucial in understanding the blue ocean of communicative leadership and the big potential of a job market for Listening Leaders. The contribution of Heike Kummer, an experienced and mindful senior HR development manager, rounded up the input from the personnel side.

With Ulrich Bauhofer, the doctor who initiated me to Transcendental Meditation, we discuss matters of leadership and this book benefited from many of his insights. Another supreme listener.

Many senior practitioners of corporate communications became engaging and precious sparring partners for communicative leadership and lots of discussions contributed to refining this concept. There are many, I limit myself to mention Jörg Allgäuer, Simone Bemporad, Martin Bendrich, Nick Boakes, Peter Dietlmaier, Celine Ducher, Richard Edelman, Jörg Eigendorf, Matthias Fritton, Richard Gaul, Walter Glogauer, Christine Graeff, Felix Gress, Armin Guhl, Thomas Knipp, Hartmut Knüppel, Klaus Kocks, Hubertus Kuelps, Cornelia Kunze, Christian Lawrence, Thibault Leclerc, Richard Lips, Michael Matern, Bernhard Meising, Bob Peterson, Elisabeth Ramelsberger, Clas Röhl, Giovanni Sanfelice di Monteforte, Oliver Santen, Matteo Scaravelli, Monika Schaller, Ilja-Kristin Seewald, Luca Virgilio, Thomas Weber, Christoph Zemelka and the young but very alert PR shooting stars Kristina Nikolayeva in Kiew and Katie Sheppet in Melbourne.

Roland Schatz and Matthias Vollbracht from Media Tenor closely observed the birth of communicative leadership and gave it the support of solid media analysis. Our discussions on crises, crisis prevention and the trust meltdown of the financial crises were constantly triggering experiments and further research. Without them and my friends Fred Reichheld and Andreas Dullweber from Bain & Co. the correlation between employee engagement and media work and profitable growth wouldn't have been identified. This is at the core of the corporate communications practice of communicative leadership, of the yin yang between business and communications.

Toni Concina and Flavia Timperi, two top communicators living in Orvieto, gave the right professional stimulus to my writing in Umbria.

Two friends, one slightly older the other much younger than me, suffered the pain of reading early drafts: Hans-Peter Martin, bestselling author, former *Spiegel* correspondent and member of the European Parliament for two legislatures and the brilliant talent Jonathan Sierck, who is in his early twenties but has already written a remarkable book on leadership and is doing his PhD dissertation on another aspect of leadership. Thank you to both of you, you were merciful in style and precise like surgeons in your critical reading.

Lena-Sophie von Schorlemer, a bright Brown and London Schools of Economics graduate pointed us to Everlane, the company mentioned in Chapter 1.

My brother Fabrizio, a banker for more than two decades, is a constant inspiration on leadership issues and an intense listener.

In the months I was writing the book the exchange with Carolin Amann, Maria Borner, Lutz Golsch, Martin Kothè, Oliver Müller, Hans Nagl,

Michael Reinert, Victoria Gräfin Strachwitz and Hartmut Vennen from FTI Consulting was as challenging as it can get. In which kind of companies will communicative leadership work? Who are the C-suite managers eligible to become Listening Leaders? Without this sanity check, this book would have been more naïve.

Björn Edlund, Gary Sheffer and Roger Bolton from Arthur Page Society as well as Jean Valin from the Global Alliance on Public Relations left their marks in this book through their research, their professional experience and the joint workshop we organised on communicative leadership and the many pleasant discussions on the matter which we entertained in the past year.

A source of constant inspiration since 1979 is my mentor Piero Bassetti, who, well beyond 80, is still a sharp observer and a superb listener.

The patience of my family was legendary. Of those directly involved in writing the book, like my daughter Clementina: I enjoyed every moment of our discussions before and for the book. Like those with her mother Lucia, who translated our book into the illustrations you find at the beginning of most chapters. Or the hefty discussions on the merits of the book, like my second daughter Fiammetta – a fresh business administration graduate from the University of Kent and my wife Heidi, a communications manager for a financial services company. Or the patience of my three-year-old son Fabio who accepted that Daddy couldn't read him books because he had to write one.

Clementina's first thanks go to the large number of fellow millennials who, in animated discussions and interviews and through their observational and introspective skills, gave her their perspective on every issue in this book. They include Viola Pagnoni and her colleagues from Methodos, Lena-Sophie von Schorlemer, Alexa Völker, Giulia Röder, Emanuele Visconti, Angelica Riccardi, Iacopo Taddeo, Flaminia Forneris, Assia Vignanelli Zichella, Lucrezia Papillo, Britta Biagi, Lisa Uttinger.

Two fellow professors have inspired and supported her. The first was Professor Alan Lewis, at the University of Bath, who opened her mind to how psychological insights can be applied to wider societal issues and macro-economy. The second is Dr Annika Nübold from Maastricht University, whose professional and personal interest in authentic leadership and mindfulness drove her curiosity in the mechanisms behind effective leadership.

A deep thanks also goes to Clementina's former boss at social media consultancy SoMazi, Maz Nadjm, who taught her about the power of social media, and to Roland Schatz for illuminating her at the Media Tenor Reputation Lab during the World Economic Forum with some highly interesting points about mistrust in organisations and where it stems from. Clementina would also here like to acknowledge family friend Sandra dal Borgo for talking to her about the importance of lack of judgement in leadership.

Gratitude goes to Fiammetta, her sister, for humbling Clementina down when she was trying too hard to be witty when writing, and for challenging some views on millennials. A big thank you goes to Lucia, her mother, for teaching her comprehension and diplomacy, both virtues of a great leader.

Last, but evidently not least, our joint and full gratitude goes to Eloise Cook from Pearson who patiently guided us through the writing and editing process. For non-native English writers like us this wasn't only a great editing experience it was also a pleasant experience of English humour and intellectual wit.

The episodes in the book are all true stories. Most of them have been 'disguised' by changing details that would make them recognisable, but keeping the true story within alive.

Emilio and Clementina Galli Zugaro, June 2016

Publisher's acknowledgements

We are grateful to the following for permission to reproduce copyright material:

Author photo on page vii © oliversoulas.com; Figure I.1 reprinted courtesy of Edelman; Figure 7.2 reprinted courtesy of Allianz SE; all illustrations created by Lucia Fabiani.

Index

trust
    accept and admit mistakes 9
    accept regulation and feedback as
        necessary control mechanisms 9
    always set the example 7–8
    build and cultivate long-term
        relationships 8
    credible sources of
        information 5–6
    EMMA (empathy, motivation,
        mentality, analysis) 8
    have consideration and respect
        for partners, competitors and
        stakeholders 9
    loss of trust in companies 2, 3–4
    and proof of reliability 8
    and provision of meaningful
        information 40–1
    say what you think and do what
        you say 9–10
    ten commandments of 7–11
    treat others as you would like to
        be treated 10–11
    triangle of competence, integrity
        and motivation 8
    walk the talk 8

United Airlines 5

Van Linge, Thomas 205
Via character test 115
viral change management 159
visual stimulation, scribing 110–11
Volkswagen 102

WABC coaches 129
Watzlawick, Paul 154
weak signals of the market and
    stakeholders 73
webcasts 47
White, Paul 96
whitewashing 76
Whitmore, Sir John 129
Wikileaks 36–7
Wilson, Meena Surie 102
work–life integration 172–3
    millennial view 173–5
World Economic Forum,
    Davos 111

YouTube 17, 47

Záboji, Peter 57–8